AN ANVIL ORIGINAL
Under the general editorship of Louis L. Snyder

BASIC HISTORY OF MODERN GERMANY

LOUIS L. SNYDER

Professor of History
The City College of New York

KRIEGER PUBLISHING COMPANY
MALABAR, FLORIDA

To
Mary, Irene, Charles, Nemo, Faye, Rosalie,
and Harold Snyder

Original Edition 1957
Reprint Edition 1980

Printed and Published by
KRIEGER PUBLISHING COMPANY
KRIEGER DRIVE
MALABAR, FLORIDA 32950

Copyright © 1957 by
Louis L. Snyder
Reprinted by Arrangement with
D. VAN NOSTRAND COMPANY, INC.

Library of Congress Cataloging in Publication Data

Snyder, Louis Leo, 1907-
    Basic history of modern Germany.

    Reprint of the edition published by Van Nostrand, New
York, issued in series: An Anvil original.
    Includes index.
    1. Germany—History.   2. Germany—History—Sources.
I. Title.
[DD175.S58 1980]   943   80-12659
ISBN 0-89874-203-X

10   9   8   7   6   5   4   3

PREFACE

THE history of Germany has been called the story of an unending struggle of the continental Teutons for a working compromise between uniformity and disruption. Such is the theme of this Anvil book—a story of dichotomy, particularism, divergency. For a thousand years the Germans sought for some golden mean between centralism and anarchy. So striking were the divisions of German history that until 1871 there was in fact no political unit called "Germany"; one should speak of the "Germanies" before that date.

In this respect Germany has never been a typically European nation. She has played a unique role in European and world history. The waves of the French Revolution covered most of Europe, but the effects on the Germanies were negligible. The Western ideals of liberty, equality, and fraternity did not take firm root in German soil; instead, the option of German rulers was for Eastern authoritarianism with a thin veneer of Western constitutionalism. The twin currents of liberalism and democracy were overwhelmed in the Germanies and in Germany by the forces of nationalism and militarism.

An attempt has been made here to present the essentials of German history without overburdening the reader with details. The book is designed primarily as an introduction to the study of German history. The readings in Part II, in conformity with the general idea of the Anvil series, have been selected to illustrate the major points of the text. Limitations of space prevent the presentation of many of these documents *in toto*, but in most cases the important ideas have been extracted.

New York City   LOUIS L. SNYDER

TABLE OF CONTENTS

Part I

THE COURSE OF MODERN GERMAN HISTORY

1. INTRODUCTION

The Land. Germany, geographically the heartland of Central Europe, has never known well-defined natural frontiers. The British have been identified with a great island, the Italians with a peninsula, and the French with sharp seacoast boundaries; but the Germans always have had artificial and impermanent frontiers. German boundaries have alternately expanded and contracted like bellows in reaction to war, colonization, purchase, exchange, and royal marriage. Germany is split up more than any other European country by numerous mountain ranges, valleys, plateaus, ridges, bays, lakes, and rivers. The North German Plain is intersected by four rivers—the Rhine, Elbe, Oder, and Vistula. From the days of the particularistic units of the Middle Ages through unification in 1871 to the present day, Germany has been burdened by an unfavorable geographical structure, without natural frontiers, and split apart instead of bound together. Lasting peculiarities of localism, regionalism, and sectionalism have resulted from this geographical fragmentation.

The People. There is no such thing as a German "race." The nation that one day was to adopt racialism as an official state policy is composed of the most varied ethnic components. In the veins of the German flows the blood of Ostrogoths, Visigoths, Vandals, Burgundians, perhaps even the Mongol-Tatar Huns. Bavarians, Angles, Saxons, Jutes, and Lombards contributed their share. The "racial purity" of the German was considerably complicated by intermarriage of his ancestors with Alamans, Franks, Swabians, and Frisians. Saxon barbarians, largely Slavic, survived Charlemagne's religious massacres. Norsemen, Muslims, and Slavs who helped disrupt the Carolingian Empire, Mongolians who

7

invaded Silesia in the thirteenth century, pagan Wends
who felt the lash of the Teutonic Knights, Poles who
were incorporated into late-eighteenth-century Prussia,
Alsatians and Lorrainers taken into the German Empire
in 1871, Jews who intermarried with Germans—all
these helped produce a people that is ethnically one of
the most mixed in Europe. The German people may be
distinguished as a linguistic and cultural entity, certainly
not as a pure "Aryan," "Nordic," or "Indo-European"
"race." (*See Reading No. 1.*)

Dualism in German History. There have been
many bitter discords in German history—political, religious, cultural, economic, and psychological. Historically, Germany has been ravaged by conflict from both
within and outside her borders. Throughout the Middle
Ages and well into modern times there were bloody feuds
among the German aristocracy. The religious wars of
the sixteenth century left a trail of slaughter; in the
Thirty Years' War of the seventeenth century the Germanies suffered great damage and the population was
substantially reduced. By the eighteenth century the
impetus for subduing the other German territories by
force came from Prussia, which sought to impress upon
Germany a special kind of unity that was the reverse of
a thousand years of German history. The Napoleonic
system of interference in the Germanies was bolstered by
the sword. Bismarck achieved the national unification of
Germany in 1871 by means of a policy of iron and blood.
Germany's drive for a place in the sun in 1914 and again
in 1939 was carried on in this tradition of violence.

The outstanding facts of German history are a
polarity of development and a dichotomy of ideas and
procedures that have never been resolved. The history
of the Germans has been the story of struggle for a
working compromise between uniformity and disruption.
Uniformity was and is contrary to the ethnic, political,
and cultural divergences of the Germans. At no time in
German history has there been one central power strong
enough to crush the centrifugal tendencies of the com-
ponent parts. At no time were the individual parts weak
enough to allow themselves to be merged in one highly
centralized body, with the exception of the short-lived

Hitler Reich. In the words of a British historian, A. J. P. Taylor:

> The history of the Germans is a history of extremes. It contains everything except moderation, and in the course of a thousand years the Germans have experienced everything except normality. They have dominated Europe, and they have been the helpless victims of the domination of others; they have enjoyed liberties unparalleled in Europe and they have fallen victims to despotisms equally without parallel; they have produced the most transcendental philosophers, the most spiritual musicians, and the most ruthless and unscrupulous politicians. 'German' has meant at one moment a being so sentimental, so trusting, so pious, as to be too good for this world; and at another a being so brutal, so unprincipled, so degraded, as to be not fit to live. Both descriptions are true; both types of Germans have existed not only at the same epoch, but in the same person. Only the normal person, not particularly good, not particularly bad, healthy, sane, moderate—he has never set his stamp on German history. Geographically the people of the center, the Germans have never found a middle way of life, either in their thought or least of all in their politics. One looks in vain in their history for a *juste milieu,* for common sense—the two qualities which have distinguished France and England. Nothing is normal in German history except violent oscillations.[1]

Superimposed on the duality of centralism versus particularism was an even greater dichotomy—the conflict between national unity and theocratical world-monarchy. While England and France emerged in early modern times as unified national states, in the Germanies there persisted a fruitless pursuit of an idealistic world-empire. Still another example of the fatal dualism in German history is the religious conflict between Protestantism and Catholicism. Whereas most of the nations of Europe chose one religion or the other during and after the Reformation, the Germanies were permanently divided religiously—Lutheran Germany and Catholic Ger-

[1] A. J. P. Taylor, *The Course of German History* (New York, 1946) p. 1.

many went their separate ways. The urge to dichotomy appeared again in the nineteenth-century struggle when Austria and Prussia attempted to dominate all Germany. Once German unity had been fashioned in the crucible of Bismarck's wars, and once the empire of William II felt itself ready for expansion, it might have been expected that the tragic dichotomy would be resolved. But not so. This time Germany was caught between the West and the East (*Drang nach Osten*). Bismarck sought a solution in a kind of halfhearted combination between Western constitutionalism and Eastern authoritarianism. Prussia, the state of soldiers and officials, became the determining factor in German history.

In no other European country did this historical cleavage reach such enormous proportions. The effect on the German people was tragic in its implications. German greatness of purpose and achievement were combined with a vague, romantic foolhardiness. The trend toward division made the Germans either frivolous or ruthless, or else they took refuge in philosophy and mysticism because the world seemed too harsh for them. Some observers deny the occurrence of traditional patterns in German history. Lawrence K. Frank says:

> One of the major difficulties of Germany is the lack of a coherent and emotionally acceptable history; the German people are dangerous because they have no consistent traditions, but rather they reach into the past for whatever rule and sanction seem desirable or expedient at the moment. Obviously such a people will alternate between Beethoven and Bismarck, between the extremes of high ethical and artistic endeavors and the worst cruelty and ruthlessness, depending upon the circumstances and the exigencies or opportunities they face.[2]

From the viewpoint of national character there seems to be a striking divergency between individual and mass reactions of Germans, an attitude recognized by the perceptive Goethe: "The Germans—so worthy as individuals, so miserable in the mass!"

Catastrophe in German History.   All nations at one time or another have been faced with imminent collapse.

[2] In *Psychiatry: Journal of the Biology and Pathology of Interpersonal Relations,* VII (1944) 231-36.

But the course of German history reveals an inordinate number of breakdowns. In 1250 the Hohenstaufen dream of world domination was shattered; when the claims of this proud medieval family were extinguished, there began the so-called *kaiserlose schreckliche Zeit,* the terrible interregnum without an emperor. The end of the Thirty Years' War saw the Germanies in decline, the government weakened, and the populace victimized by dynastic ambitions and religious prejudices. In 1803 the Empire was once again smashed, this time under the Napoleonic heel. The ignominious failure of the Frankfort Assembly of 1848 meant the eclipse of Western liberalism in the Germanies, and German national aspirations toward freedom—toward democracy and parliamentarianism—disappeared in the presence of Prussian militarism and "the tranquillity of the graveyard." After Bismarck achieved German national unification and William II set Germany on a New Course as a world power, German arms collapsed in 1918 on the battlefield. Once more the nation disintegrated internally. The catastrophe of 1945 meant for Germany unconditional surrender, temporary suspension of the sovereignty of the German nation, and occupation by armies representing varied political and economic ideologies.

There seems to be a kind of fateful rhythm in this series of calamities and disasters, which Veit Valentin terms "a unique picture of historical tragedy *in excelsis.*" It is a tribute, perhaps, to the staying power of the German people to say that again and again they have survived one terrible blow after another in the course of their erratic historical development.

Early History of the Germanies.   The history of Germany begins with the division of the Carolingian Empire into three parts among the grandsons of Charlemagne by the Treaty of Verdun (843). (*See Readings Nos. 2 and 3.*) Louis the German (843-876) was unable to fashion an ordered society in the East Frankish (German) kingdom after the destruction caused by the new barbarian invasions of Moravians and Hungarians. When, in 911, the East Frankish line of the Carolingian dynasty died out, there was a vicious struggle for political control as the dukes of Bavaria, Swabia, Franconia, and Lorraine, as well as hundreds of lesser lords of the stem-duchies, resisted any attempts to infringe upon their independence. Any bearer of the German crown was confronted with the double hostility of regionalism and tribalism.

This urge to centralization persisted in the medieval Germanies due to the efforts of a series of dynasties—the Ottonians, the Franconians, the Hohenstaufens, and the Hapsburgs—to bring about some kind of unity. Otto I (936-973), the first of the Ottonian (Saxon) dynasty, was able to make the Germanies one of the foremost powers in Europe. Crowned at Rome in 962 by Pope John XII as Holy Roman Emperor, Otto sought to make himself the successor of Augustus, Constantine, and Charlemagne. This attempt to re-create the Roman Empire under Germanic auspices was doomed to failure. Subsequent German kings also tried to forge unity among the particularistic German duchies and at the same time control all Italy and dominate the papacy, but none was successful. Each time a German king set out on a campaign in the Italies, he had to fight his way through North Italy and then seek to smash his way back home. The area of Lombardy is filled with the bones of Germans slain in these ineffectual operations.

The central authority remained vague and undefined. Otto's successor, Otto II (973-983), finding the difficulties of his position unsurmountable, was unable to conquer southern Italy. Otto III (983-1002) likewise attempted to expand the German state, but his ambitions brought him into direct conflict with the German princes and the papacy. Henry II (1002-1024) contented himself with governing the Germanies.

The Franconian dynasty ruled the Germanies for more than a century. Since there was no direct heir upon the death of Henry II in 1024, Conrad of Franconia was elected by the princes. Conrad II (1024-1039) suppressed rebellions in the Italies and annexed Burgundy (1033). His son Henry III (1039-1056) extended German influence over Slavic areas and Hungary and preserved domestic peace by maintaining the royal authority over both nobility and clergy. The youthful Henry IV, who ascended the throne in 1056, was unable to maintain authority over the papacy and yielded important prerogatives to Gregory VII in the investiture struggle.

The attempt of the Hohenstaufen dynasty—"the

most brilliant failures of the Middle Ages"—to consolidate the strength of the Empire at the expense of the
papacy was likewise unsuccessful. Conrad III (1138-
1152), the first of the Hohenstaufens, and Frederick I
Barbarossa (1152-1190), were unable to subdue the
rebellious northern Italian city-states, nor did the later
Hohenstaufens—Henry VI (1190-1197), Frederick II
(1212-1250), and Conrad IV (1250-1254)—succeed in
breaking the temporal power of the papacy. Despite its
failure, the reign of the Hohenstaufen dynasty is regarded by Germans as one of the most glorious periods
of their history. The Hohenstaufens, termed a "viper
brood" by the papacy, did not achieve unity, but they
promoted German expansion, increased colonization in
the northeast, and encouraged the development of urban
life.

After the death of the last Hohenstaufen in 1254,
there was a period of chaos, the Great Interregnum, lasting until 1273. With the decline of the central power,
such strong independent houses as the Luxemburgs, Hapsburgs, and Hohenzollerns each sought to consolidate its
position as the leading power in the Germanies. In this
period of disunity, the Age of *Faustrecht* (fist law),
each local district depended upon its own strength for
security.

In 1273 Rudolf of Hapsburg was elected to the imperial dignity. Rudolf vigorously suppressed the feuds
between local barons and knights and established a sem-
blance of royal authority. He abandoned the Italian
peninsula and sought to consolidate his German realm.
Freed from the necessity of sending a constant stream of
men and supplies to the south to maintain a shadowy
imperial pretense, he was able to strengthen his position
in the Germanies.

Nevertheless, the breakdown in imperial authority was
legally recognized in the next century by an important
constitutional document. The independent princes, the
great ecclesiastics, and the league of German cities all
resisted any increase in royal authority. From Charles
IV of Luxemburg (1347-1378), the princes and ecclesiastics were successful in extracting a document, the
Golden Bull (1356), which defined and increased the
powers of the prince electors and which, in effect, became

the constitution of the medieval empire. By this instrument the Holy Roman Emperor was to be chosen by
seven electors: four lay princes—the king of Bohemia,
the duke of Saxony, the count palatine of the Rhine, and
the margrave of Brandenburg—and three ecclesiastics—
the archbishops of Mayence, Cologne, and Trier. The
election was to take place at Frankfort-on-Main and the
coronation was to be held at Aix-la-Chapelle (Aachen).
There was to be no papal interference in the elections.
This epoch-making imperial law effectively froze the
sovereign position of the electors and perpetuated the
internal divisions in the Germanies. (*See Reading No.
4.*) Broken again into small, independent states, the
Germanies degenerated once more into feudal chaos. A
compact German Empire, extending to the waters of the
Dnieper and the Gulf of Bothnia, might have been
fashioned early in German history, but instead, the German monarchs squandered their energies in relentless and
unsuccessful pursuit of a vague, shadowy ideal.

From the thirteenth century down to the Napoleonic
era there was no Germany in a political sense, but only
a great number of virtually independent states, some large,
some small. The most important Hapsburg leaders, Maxi-
milian I (1493-1519) and Charles V (1519-1556), still
pursued the dream of acquiring control over the Italies;
they were unsuccessful either because their interests were
elsewhere or because the local German princes were too
powerful. While English and French monarchs were
consolidating strong national unions, the Germanies
remained an aggregation of weak, squabbling states.

Austria was the nominal head at this time of the
Holy Roman Empire, which had at best only a theoretical
unity. The disruptive force of the Reformation weakened
the control of the Catholic emperors over the Protestant
German states. The revolt against Rome in the Germanies
sprang from resentment against the papacy, which, as a
tried and fixed policy, always supported the particularistic
lords against the German emperor as a means of preventing national German unity. (*See Reading No. 5.*)
Luther gave the Germans a consciousness of national
existence, but at the same time contributed heavily to
the dualism of German history. He broke with the
medieval dream of universalism, only to lead the German

people once more into the quagmire of particularism. Lutheranism began by eliminating papal influence in the north of Germany, but leadership promptly fell into the hands of the princes. Lutheranism, accepted by only half the German population, made its way among the princes of the North Sea and Baltic area, while Bavaria, in the southwest, and in the Rhineland the princes and people remain loyal to Rome. It was a permanent split.

In the Thirty Years' War (1618-1648) the German princes, helped by Denmark, Sweden, and France, successfully resisted the imperial power. The Treaty of Westphalia (1648), depriving the Holy Roman emperor of his powers over the German principalities, marked the end of imperial efforts to unify the Germanies. Freed from centralized control, the petty princes were left again to their own devices. By 1800 the Germanies took on the quality of a "geographical expression," consisting of 314 states and 1,475 estates, a total of 1,789 independent sovereign powers. Many kings, dukes, and margraves attempted with a limited budget to create their courts on the majestic model of Louis XIV's Versailles. The development of a normal, healthy nationalism out of this crazy-quilt pattern was, perhaps, too much to expect. Whereas feudalism was broken in other Western European countries, it lingered on for several additional centuries in the conglomerate Germanies.

-- 2 --

THE RISE OF PRUSSIA

The Nuclei of Prussia. Three small separated territories in northern Germany were eventually joined together to form the nucleus of the Brandenburg-Prussian state: Brandenburg in the center, between the Elbe and the Oder; Prussia, in the east, along the Baltic; and the

Cleves-Mark inheritance on the Lower Rhine. During the latter part of the reign of Otto the Great in the tenth century, border provinces, or marks, had been established along the whole eastern frontier of the Holy Roman Empire as bulwarks against the Slavs. One of these marks, Brandenburg, a remote frontier state on sandy wastes, had been carved out as a feudal domain by the crusading Teutonic knights, who had either exterminated or converted the Slavs in the area. The margrave of Brandenburg was the least important of the Seven Electors who traditionally elected the emperor of the Holy Roman Empire and whose positions were legalized by the Golden Bull of 1356. After some five centuries of separate existence, Brandenburg, Prussia, and Cleves-Mark were united in a personal union under John Sigismund, Elector of Brandenburg (1608-1619). Together with fresh territory, these three lands emerged to form the Frederician State and the basis of the Bismarckian Empire. There was no "growth" of Prussia in the accepted sense, for she represented no popular force, and she scarcely belonged to Germany, either geographically or culturally. Her lone and decisive asset was a sense of ruthless power acquired in the long process of dominating the Slavic peoples. But it was Prussia that impressed upon the remainder of the Germanies a pattern of traditions and ideals that came to be recognized as universally German.

The Hohenzollern Dynasty.   The ancestral home of the Zollerns was a Swabian castle near the Danube and the Neckar, just north of Switzerland. In 1170 Conrad of Hohenzollern left his home to seek his fortune by serving under Frederick Barbarossa. Two centuries later, one of Conrad's descendants was invested with the sovereignty of Brandenburg. Displaying its symbolic emblem—"From the Mountains to the Sea"—the Hohenzollern family began to play a role in Northern Germany comparable to that of the Hapsburgs in the South. To consolidate and increase their territories by acquiring intermediate lands became the steady goal of the Hohenzollerns. Brandenburg emerged as an important Protestant state in the religious wars following the Reformation. During the seventeenth century the Hohenzollerns became wealthy by confiscating Catholic properties. Under

Frederick the Great (1740-1786) the consolidated Kingdom of Prussia became one of the chief states of Europe.

The Junkers. The emergence of Prussia was an outgrowth of a union of the Hohenzollern dynasty and a noble squirearchy of bellicose Junkers. Brandenburg, an area of savagery and conquest, had been dominated by a ruthless, arrogant, ignorant nobility, many of whom were of Slavic origin. These Junkers—the name is derived from *junc-herre* (young lord)—were great landed nobles who understood the arts of war and efficient administration. From their ranks came many of the generals, statesmen, and businessmen who played an important part in later German historical development. The Prussian Junkers have been described aptly as barbarians who had learned to handle a rifle, and, still more, bookkeeping by double entry. Politically, they remained in a primitive stage, but economically and administratively they look forward to the era of the Industrial Revolution.

From the political, social, and economic disturbances that accompanied the making of modern Germany, the Junkers emerged as the dominant ruling and governing social class. They learned, as Frederick William I had hoped, "to recognize no leaders other than God and the King of Prussia." Combining physical courage with a worship of the sword, political knowledge with cruelty and brutality, tenacity with arrogance, the Junkers exhibited an extraordinary capacity to endure under any circumstances. Always mercenary and always selfish, they identified the national interests of Germany with their own. When the new industrial and financial aristocracy of Western and Southern Germany attained a position of power, it soon became amalgamated with the Junkers. In the process the Junkers were able to smooth off the rough edges of their Eastern heritage.

Allied with three Hohenzollern rulers, the Junkers fashioned absolutism and militarism into a social system that made them its chief beneficiaries. They took advantage of every historical movement—nationalism, liberalism, imperialism, capitalism, even socialism—all of which they used shrewdly to make their own position in the social order more secure and more dominant. Although they declined somewhat in economic importance during the nineteenth and twentieth centuries, the Junkers were able to weather every political, military, and economic storm—the War of Liberation in 1806-07, the crises of 1848-49, 1862-66, 1870-71, and 1878-79, the collapse of 1918, the Weimar Republic, and even Nazi Germany. Again and again they outwitted their rivals, and emerged from the struggle rejuvenated and intact as a governing class and as a political power. Seldom in history has there been a better example of how one vital element can profoundly influence the entire social order of a nation. The Junker ideals of *Realpolitik,* military power, patriotism, materialism, respect for order, and public service were impressed indelibly on the German body politic. German nationalism became thoroughly tinged with the Junker spirit—ironically by a spirit that once had opposed national unification, but, characteristically, had become reconciled to it.

The Great Elector, Frederick William (1640-1688). Efficiency and order were brought to Brandenburg by Frederick William, called the Great Elector. While increasing the area of his dominions (Eastern Pomerania in 1648 as a reward for his part in the Thirty Years' War, the renunciation of Polish sovereignty over East Prussia in 1660, and definite establishment of his title to Cleves and Ravensburg in 1666), he at the same time showed remarkable skill as an administrator. As a youth he had spent four years at the University of Leyden in the Netherlands, where he had imbibed Western ideas. As ruler he centralized the administration of Brandenburg, organized a Council of State, devised the financial system, encouraged commerce, industry, and agriculture, constructed the Frederick William Canal joining the Oder to a branch of the Elbe and thereby creating an outlet to the North Sea, augmented educational facilities, and replaced his once undisciplined troops with an efficient and disciplined national force. After the revocation by Louis XIV of the Edict of Nantes in 1685, the Great Elector welcomed to his country more than twenty thousand Huguenots, whose skill and industry contributed strongly to the prosperity of his state. He justified his absolute rule on the ground that it brought unity, strength, and order. At his accession he had found a state with many of its villages deserted, its agriculture at a standstill, its landowners and peasants impoverished, its commerce and industry almost non-existent, and its intellectual life demoralized. Affairs in Brandenburg were so well managed by Frederick William that at his death the state was enjoying great prosperity.

Frederick I (1688-1713). The son of the Great Elector lacked the qualities of his father. "Great in small things, and small in great things," he allowed some of the work accomplished by his father to be undone. Disturbed by the fact that he possessed no royal title, Frederick III, Elector of Brandenburg and Duke of Prussia, was determined to obtain one. It was said that he had been deeply humiliated when in an interview with William III of England he was obliged to sit in a chair without arms while the British monarch was comfortably seated in a magnificent armchair. By tradition it was necessary to obtain the consent of his liege lord, the Holy Roman Emperor, Leopold I, for a royal title. An opportunity came in 1700, just preceding the War of the Spanish Succession, when the Emperor required Frederick's support. In 1701 Leopold granted him the coveted dignity, but made the title read Frederick I, King *in* Prussia, thus sparing the feelings of the king of Poland, who still ruled West Prussia, and at the same time making it clear that Prussia lay outside the boundaries of the Holy Roman Empire. Subsequent Prussian kings changed the title to King *of* Prussia.

Frederick William I (1713-1740). The next Prussian monarch, Frederick William I, inaugurated the policy of building up an efficient army and a subservient bureaucracy. A man of phenomenal energy and violent temper, Frederick William consolidated and centralized his government, practiced rigid economy, and encouraged the development of commerce and industry. With little education himself, he nevertheless felt its importance and founded several hundred elementary schools. Miserly in other respects, he never hesitated to spend state funds lavishly for military purposes. His chief pride and his one great extravagance was to acquire tall soldiers, paying high prices for them and obtaining the giants wherever he could in Europe. Though he did not use this efficient army for territorial aggrandizement, he gave his son the means for making Prussia one of the first states of Europe.

Frederick the Great (1740-1786). Frederick II as crown prince was an effeminate young man who detested the endless drills and monotonous service to which he was subjected. His irascible parent imposed an iron discipline upon him. From this hard education the young Frederick emerged sobered and cured of his follies, but embittered and skeptical. To the surprise of many who had known him when he was younger, he developed into an unscrupulous war lord and a master of statecraft. (*See Reading No. 6.*) Building on the foundations laid by his predecessors, he raised his small and comparatively poor kingdom to a position of first-rate military importance. He asserted his equality with the Emperor, made Prussia the one important rival of Austria in the Germanies, and virtually forced his nation into the ranks of the Great Powers. He made Prussia great, but in the process he further assured German disunity. "By his cult of military force and by his own example of military success," says Koppel S. Pinson, "he implanted in Prussia, and through Prussia in Germany, that inordinate reliance on military strength which both the Germany of Bismarck and the Germany of Hitler were to follow. He became the supreme example of the amoral national hero who hovered over and above the everyday concepts of good and evil." [3]

Acceding to the throne in 1740 at the age of 28, Frederick promptly made use of his small but efficient army of 80,000 men. He was determined to claim from the Empress of Austria the four Silesian duchies which had been lost in the Thirty Years' War. The empress categorically refused. Without a declaration of war, without any moral or legal right for his action, Frederick invaded and annexed the Austrian province of Silesia. The issue was complicated by conflicting claims to the Austrian heritage: before his death, the Holy Roman Emperor, Charles VI, had obtained the promise of all the European states, with the exception of Bavaria, to recognize his daughter Maria Theresa as queen of the Austrian dominions (Pragmatic Sanction). Emboldened by Frederick's coup, Bavaria, supported by France, Spain, and Saxony, began the War of the Austrian Succession (1740-1748). Frederick entered and withdrew from the struggle several times. By 1748 all parties were thoroughly weary of the

[3] Koppel S. Pinson, *Modern Germany* (New York, 1954) p. 6.

war. According to the Peace of Aix-la-Chapelle, Maria Theresa was recognized as ruler of all the Hapsburg lands, but Prussia retained Silesia.

During eight years of uneasy peace there was a diplomatic revolution, designed to throttle the Prussian king. Austria and France, convinced now that Frederick was a menace, signed a secret treaty, to which Russia, Poland, Sweden, and Saxony also subscribed, by which it was agreed to divide Prussia among them. England, whose interests in North America were threatened by French trade and colonization, promised to help Prussia. The resulting Seven Years' War (1756-1763) was world-wide in scope. Hostilities between England and France began in India (1751) and in North America (1754). Faced with an overwhelming coalition and almost sure destruction, but certain that his best defense lay in striking swiftly, Frederick began the war in Europe in 1756, winning two brilliant victories at Rossbach and Leuthen (1757). These astonishing triumphs brought Silesia back to Frederick; he was hailed as one of the greatest military geniuses in history. The city of London was illuminated in his honor, and the English Parliament voted him $3,500,000 a year, which it discontinued a few years later. Then followed a long series of disasters as Frederick sought to drag the war along, to exhaust and separate his opponents. In 1759 he suffered a stunning defeat by the Russians and Austrians at Kunersdorf. In 1760 Frederick was at bay, with 200,000 bayonets goading him from all sides. He was rescued from this predicament by what he later called a miracle—the death of his relentless enemy, the Czarina Elizabeth in January, 1762. Her successor, Peter III, a warm admirer of Frederick, not only made peace with him but sent an army to help him. The enemy coalition evaporated. The Peace of Hubertusburg (1763) required Frederick to evacuate occupied Saxony, but he was permitted to retain Silesia. Although Prussia had gained no new territory, she was now hailed as a Great Power in the Germanies and Eastern Europe.

Frederick II returned from the Seven Years' War an old man but still buoyant in spirit. Prussia having been wasted and weakened by the terrible struggle, Frederick now set about the task of repairing the enormous damage. Since many of his hardiest soldiers had fallen in the war, he induced tens of thousands of colonists to settle in his dominions and he founded some 500 villages. He reduced the taxes on free farmers, but did not abolish serfdom. He allowed the nobles to retain their large holdings, but required them to rebuild thousands of ruined farmhouses. He reclaimed vast areas of farm lands by draining swamps and building levees, and introduced the cultivation of the potato as a cheap article of food, despite riots against the measure arising from the legend that potatoes caused leprosy and fevers. Pursuing a mercantilist policy, he encouraged commerce and industry, prevented the flow of money from Prussia, levied duties on foreign imports, and nourished home industries. He constructed roads and waterways including a canal connecting a tributary of the Oder with the Vistula River.

An enlightened despot, nourished by his faith in God and Voltaire, Frederick regarded himself as the first servant of the state. "The people," he said, "are not here for the sake of the rulers, but the rulers for the sake of the people." He regulated every conceivable administrative matter in the most minute detail, and filled the public positions with faithful servants, all inspired by his dictum that idleness was akin to death. He restored the Academy of Sciences, promoted elementary education, remodeled the judicial system, and granted toleration to both Catholics and Protestants. Eighteenth-century rationalists regarded him as a kind of successful demigod.

Frederick the Great died on August 17, 1786, at the age of 74. His reign marked the culmination of the development of Brandenburg-Prussia from a weak electorate to one of the strongest military states in Europe. The following figures show the extraordinary progress of the state from the end of the Thirty Years' War to the death of Frederick the Great:

	1648	1740	1786
Population	750,000	2,500,000	5,000,000
Army	8,000	83,000	200,000
Annual revenue, in talers	?	7,000,000	19,000,000
Stored treasure, in talers	0	8,000,000	51,000,000

"But Prussia," Sidney B. Fay reminds us, "still remained a despotic state, such as was characteristic of the eighteenth century. Unfortunately Frederick's genius as an Enlightened Despot was not a heritable quality to be transmitted to his immediate successors. It required the shock of the Napoleonic conquest and the genius of Freiherr vom Stein to bring about a new creative period of institutional changes which were to regenerate and further strengthen Prussia in the nineteenth century." [4]

— 3 —

THE ERA OF FRENCH SUPREMACY, 1789-1815

The French Revolution. The French Revolution changed the Germanics almost as much as it altered France, though its effects were different for the east of the Rhine. In its initial stages the Revolution, with its spirit of liberty, equality, and fraternity, aroused the intense admiration of German intellectuals who hailed the era as the dawn of a better world. But as revolutionary violence increased in France and as there was a danger of French imperialistic conquest, German intellectuals saw their golden dream shattered, and turned instead to German nationalism. The vast majority of the German people were at first deeply impressed by the French revolt against tyranny and the new call for the rights of the people, but caught in the quagmire of blind obedience and discipline, they could not bring themselves, as did the French people, to revolutionary action. There was an organized revolutionary movement in the Germanies. The French people acted for themselves; the Germans waited for the benefits of a revolution without

[4] Sidney B. Fay, *The Rise of Brandenburg-Prussia to 1786* (New York, 1937) p. 142.

exerting any effort themselves. From the beginning the German rulers execrated the French Revolution as insurrection run wild, and trembled in the knowledge that the storm might break at any time in their own dominions. When it became obvious that a repetition of the French experience was not likely in the Germanies, the princes competed with one another to gain the favor of the new rulers on the Seine. The seeds of rationalism—liberalism, democracy, constitutionalism, cosmopolitanism, tolerance—did not take firm root in German soil. Caught between the ideals of the libertarian West and the authoritarian East, the Germans remained suspended in a fatal dichotomy.

The Age of Napoleon. During his tempestuous career, the Corsican adventurer played football with the kingdoms and monarchies around him. None received more merciless treatment than the German princes. Napoleon's policy was a combination of naked conquest and his desire, as a kind of political missionary, to bring his own selection of revolutionary fruits to conquered peoples. He sought to play off Austria against Prussia, allowing neither one to become dominant in the Germanies, but clearly he intended eventually to destroy the independent existence of both. A long series of French victories led the Hapsburgs to give up the imperial, German cause, and paralyzed the Hohenzollerns into inaction. Frederick William II (1786-1797) and Frederick William III (1797-1840) deserted the Empire, and very nearly saw the complete destruction of Prussia. On the principle of divide-and-rule, Napoleon built up the smaller German states at the expense of the larger. The sovereigns of Bavaria, Württemberg, Baden, and Saxony, believing it was the better part of discretion to ally themselves with the devil rather than seek to fight him, cultivated a carefully thought-out servility toward the French conqueror, and as a result reaped rich territorial and personal rewards, mostly at the expense of Austria.

Destruction of the Holy Roman Empire (1806). It was Napoleon who put an end to medieval Germany. As early as 1803 he set up a glorified real-estate office in Paris which distributed the German ecclesiastical states and free cities, with some exceptions, among the secular princes. The number of sovereign states in the Germanies was reduced to about thirty. The death blow to the Empire and the further weakening of Austria came on August 6, 1806. (*See Reading No. 7.*) Although it had in fact long ceased to exist, the Holy Roman Empire nevertheless persisted as an ideal. Napoleon now forced Francis II to lay down his imperial crown, retaining the title of Francis I, Emperor of Austria. The old Holy Roman Empire, which had been the only bond linking the Germanies together for more than eight hundred years since the imperial coronation by the pope of Otto I (962), disappeared, and the legal existence of the German states that had grown up on its territory was recognized. The Empire perished unwept, unhonored, and unsung. Thus was formalized, by Napoleonic power, the end of theocracy and feudalism in the Germanies.

Confederation of the Rhine (1806). Several weeks earlier, on July 17, 1806, Napoleon created the Confederation of the Rhine as a kind of "Third Germany" to balance the states of Prussia and Austria. Sixteen German princes, include those of Bavaria, Baden, Württemberg, Hesse-Darmstadt, and twelve smaller ones, were ordered to combine; they were given twenty-four hours to ratify the document. Though retaining control of their domestic affairs, they were required to accept Napoleon's domination of their foreign policies, and to pledge more than sixty thousand troops for the armies of France. This consolidation of the Germanies survived Napoleon's downfall, and paved the way for the national unification of Germany. Thus, a major impetus for German national unity came from the outside. On August 1, 1806, the princes of the Rhenish alliance declared their formal secession from the Holy Roman Empire, an act that helped to convince Joseph II to abdicate as emperor.

The Humiliation of Prussia. At this inopportune moment the timid poodle decided to attack the giant mastiff. Frederick William III, cautious and vacillating heretofore, allowed himself to be carried away by the war party in Berlin, and chose to challenge Napoleon at a time when the French conqueror was at the height of his power. In response to a Prussian ultimatum, Napoleon arrived in Franconia at the head of an army of

200,000 men and inflicted a disastrous defeat on Prussia at Jena and Auerstädt (October 14, 1806). The defeat threw Prussia into a wild panic as one fortress after another surrendered without firing a gun. Napoleon, entering Berlin, sent the Victory Monument on the Brandenburg Gate back to Paris. By the Peace of Tilsit (July 9, 1807) Prussia lost nearly half her territory and population and was obliged to pay an enormous indemnity. It was the most disastrous military defeat in Prussia's history.

S. H. Steinberg attributes the unprecedented defeat of Prussia to the fact that the Prussian state was a mechanical automaton without a living spirit; when a part of the machinery broke down, the whole works came to a standstill and became a useless heap of scrap. When the army and civil servants, who had been conditioned to blind obedience, no longer heard the familiar words of command, they became bewildered and only too glad to have Napoleon relieve them from the necessity of thinking for themselves.

The Regeneration of Prussia. It became clear now to Frederick William III's advisers that the only way to defeat France was to imitate her. Recognizing that the French Revolution had brought the French people a new vigor, they recommended a series of reforms that would achieve change "not through a violent impulsion from within . . . but through the wisdom of those in authority." Karl Freiherr vom Stein (1757-1831), Karl August von Hardenberg (1750-1822), and David von Scharnhorst (1755-1813) were the chief architects of reform. Stein and Hardenberg were responsible for a series of edicts emancipating the Prussian peasantry, eliminating medieval economic regulations, establishing a new system of municipal self-government, and creating a modern bureaucracy. Scharnhorst, assisted by Gneisenau and Clausewitz, reorganized the Prussian army, introducing military conscription and a reserve system on the theory that an enthusiastically patriotic army was superior to one consisting of fearful automatons. Wilhelm von Humboldt initiated educational reforms designed to increase the authority of the Prussian state. All these reforms, imposed from above and planned to strengthen Prussia, were couched in the language of liberalism, but actually were promoted to construct a state able to meet France on her own level. (*See Reading No. 8.*) "I hate the French," said Stein, "as much as it is allowed a Christian to hate." The reforms solidified militarism, produced an educational system geared as a servant of the state, and carefully avoided allowing the people any real responsibility for governing themselves. The ideal of liberty was supplanted by the ideal of authority, *die Obrigkeit.* This Prussian system was later to be welded on all Germany.

The Role of Romanticism. As as means of forgetting their degradation in the darkness of Napoleonic despotism, Germans turned their eyes backward to their great legendary past, when the old imperial Germany had been the cockpit of Europe. Seeking their salvation in romanticism, they sought to draw strength from German antiquity, from the German landscape, and from the German language, customs, and art. In contemptuous disgust they rejected their own age as barren in feeling and imagination, and preferred to steep themselves in the obscure mysticism and symbolism of the past. What they wanted was not French universalism and its concomitant of world-citizenship, but a new Germany. Some Germans were so distressed by the disgraceful submission to Napoleon that they gave up the struggle. Heinrich von Kleist, the first important dramatist after Schiller, died by his own hand on the shore of the Wannsee near Potsdam in 1811.

Others were made of sterner stuff. Their romanticism was merged with the rising spirit of German nationalism. Friedrich Ludwig Jahn (1778-1852) conceived the idea of reviving the morale of his countrymen by improving their physical condition through Swedish gymnastics. Ernst Moritz Arndt (1769-1860) expressed the new sense of nationalism in a famous poem:

> Where is the German's fatherland?
> Name me at length that mighty land!
> "Where'er resounds the German tongue,
> Where'er its hymns to God are sung."
> Be this the land,
> Brave German, this thy fatherland!

The Grimm brothers, Jakob Ludwig Karl (1785-1863) and Wilhelm Karl (1786-1859), called attention to

German national indigenous literature. Other German romantics—Tieck, Novalis, Körner, Herder, Fichte, Schelling, and Schleiermacher—contributed to the rising sense of nationalism. (*See Reading No. 9.*)

The War of Liberation (1813-1815). Invigorated by reform, Prussia concluded an alliance with Russia early in 1813 and declared war on France. Frederick William III issued a proclamation calling upon the nation to rise for their liberty and independence "in the last, decisive struggle." The response was described by Ernst Moritz Arndt in a famous passage used repeatedly in German history textbooks since that day:

> Fired with enthusiasm, the people rose, 'with God for King and Fatherland.' Among the Prussians there was only one voice, one feeling, one anger and one love, to save the Fatherland and free Germany. The Prussians wanted war; war and death they wanted; peace they feared because they could hope for no honorable peace from Napoleon.
>
> War, war, sounded the cry from the Carpathians to the Baltic, from the Niemen to the Elbe. War! cried the nobleman and landed proprietor who had become impoverished. War! the peasant who was driving his last horse to death. . . . War! the citizen who was growing exhausted from quartering soldiers and paying taxes. War! the widow who was sending her only son to the front. War! the young girl who, with tears of pride and pain, was dismissing her betrothed. Youths who were hardly able to bear arms, men with gray hair, officers who on account of wounds and mutilations had long ago been honorably discharged, rich landed proprietors and officials, fathers of large families and managers of extensive businesses were unwilling to remain behind. Even young women under all sorts of disguises rushed to arms; all wanted to drill, arm themselves and fight and die for the Fatherland.

Napoleon, describing his defeat in Russia as an accident, managed to raise an army of fresh conscripts in exhausted France and once more set about the task of subjugating his enemies. Prussian troops under Marshall Blücher (1742-1818) played an important role in the final defeats of Napoleon at Leipzig (1813) and Waterloo (1815).

— 4 —

THE RESTORATION IN THE GERMANIES: AUSTRO-PRUSSIAN PARTNERSHIP, 1815-1848

The German Confederation. The German Confederation, established at the Congress of Vienna in 1815, was a loose union of 38 sovereign states including the Austrian Empire, the Kingdoms of Prussia, Bavaria, Saxony, Württemberg, and Hanover; the Grand Duchies of Baden, Hesse-Darmstadt, Mecklenburg-Schwerin and Strelitz, Saxe-Weimar, and Oldenburg; the Electorate of Hesse-Cassel; the Duchies of Brunswick, Nassau, Saxe-Coburg-Gotha, Meiningen and Hildburghausen, Anhalt-Dessau, Bernburg, and Cöthen; Denmark (since the King of Denmark was Duke of Holstein); the Netherlands (since the King of the Netherlands was Grand Duke of Luxemburg); the four free cities of Lübeck, Bremen, Hamburg, and Frankfort-on-Main; and several small principalities. The Bundestag, or Diet, the legislative body of the Confederation (in reality a congress of ambassadors) met at Frankfort to decide questions common to all the states. No member could declare war against any other member, nor form any alliance with a foreign power that would be injurious to any one of the states. The army of the Confederation was composed of troops furnished on the basis of the population of each member and was commanded by officers appointed by the Diet.

The architects of reaction at Vienna gave Prussia a subordinate role in the German Confederation, a source of deep disappointment to Prussian patriots. The dualism between Austria and Prussia was retained, thus evading the problem of German unity. The problem of individual liberty was left to the states. In North Germany the pre-

Napoleonic princes who were restored to their thrones promptly rescinded constitutional reforms. The South German states maintained the Napoleonic system of autocratic centralized political power. The statesmen of Vienna, in the name of legitimacy, actually restored the boundaries of the old Reich, without any attention to the rising spirit of nationalism. Pursuing a policy of supranational cooperation, forced from above, they sought to turn the clock backward. They were operating in the wrong century.

Metternichian Reaction. The period from the Congress of Vienna in 1815 to the Revolution of 1848 has been described as the Age of Metternich. Count (afterward Prince) Clemens Wenzel Lothar Metternich (1773-1859), State Chancellor of Austria from 1809 to 1848, was a Rhenish aristocrat, a counterrevolutionary and conservative who hated the French Revolution, the bourgeoisie, and Napoleon with equal ardor. Convinced that he was defending the best values of civilization, he used his great powers to repress tendencies to liberty and national independence. Establishing a system of repression in Austria, he at the same time extended his measures to include Prussia. (*See Reading No. 10.*) German patriots, convinced that they had not been permitted to reap the fruits of their sacrifices, called for a free and united nation. The demand for union and freedom was especially strong in the German universities. "The Bund seemed to us," said a contemporary youth of the period, "only a police organization dedicated to the suppression of all national life." Brotherhoods of young men, called *Burschenschaften*, pledged themselves to destroy all tyrants at home and to end what they called Metternich's meddling from Vienna. On October 18, 1817, during the jubilee year of Luther's revolt, students held a great celebration at the Wartburg, during which they consigned symbols of tyranny to the flames. On March 23, 1819, a fanatical student murdered Kotzebue, a reactionary journalist suspected of being a spy in the pay of the Russian tsar. Annoyed and worried about these "insurrections," Metternich drew up the Carlsbad Decrees (1819), providing for special officials in the German universities to supervise the conduct of students and teachers, establishing a rigid press censorship, and providing for the arrest and imprisonment of vociferous German patriots.

Metternich, who considered himself the model of an enlightened rationalist and who deemed his brand of conservation to be highly desirable, understood little of the twin forces of nationalism and liberalism. A cosmopolitan, he thought in terms of a European system, in which a great Austria would counterbalance France and Russia. Above all, he wanted to frustrate any German desires for freedom and unity, on the ground that this meant a new revolution. He would cooperate with Prussia, so long as Prussia was maintained in an inferior position; German nationalism, on the other hand, was a force to be rigidly suppressed because it would upset the nice balance of Europe as Metternich conceived it.

— 5 —

GERMAN ECONOMIC AND SOCIAL LIFE AFTER 1815

The Germanies in 1815. The German Confederation in 1815 was almost entirely an agricultural area, poor and underpopulated. The population was only 26,000,000. Three-quarters of the German people lived in villages and small towns. In Prussia only Berlin, Breslau, and Königsberg numbered more than 50,000 inhabitants. Communications throughout the Confederation were in a primitive condition; many of the roads were merely paths through the forests.

The social structure in 1815 was divided into three main classes: the nobility, the educated middle class, and "the people" (the last including all those whom the middle class regarded as its inferiors—peasants, artisans, shopkeepers, domestic servants, and the proletariat). Economic life pivoted on the status of the *Bauerntum,* or peasantry. The Stein-Hardenburg reforms in Prussia in 1807, followed by other German states, gave the peasants personal freedom, but failed to regulate their property status. Big landowners demanded compensation for the loss of peasant services and draught animals. The laws of 1811 and 1816 required the peasants to give up as much as half their land to the nobility; in one Pomeranian village alone these laws drove 49 of 61 peasants from the land. Many landless peasants migrated from Eastern Germany to the western industrial towns in an effort to make a living. The feud between the big landowners and the peasantry in the west and in the south was equally bitter.

Trade and industry were still regulated by old medieval guild laws. Some traditional handicrafts remained— weaving in Silesia, toy-making in the Black Forest—but others became obsolete. Journeymen began to lose their status in the guild system, being grouped indistinguishably with vagabonds and casual workers; the hopeless journeyman became the nucleus of the new proletariat. The Germanies had no modern industries, no factories, no steam engines, no interest in sources of industrial power.

German Economic Progress, 1815-1850. Between 1815 and 1850 there was a striking change in the economic picture. "The whole German nation," says Edmond Vermeil, "seems to have swung right around on its own axis, dragging itself out of the slough of the past to create an economic system on a scale unparalleled in European history." Strongly influenced by economic liberalism and the Western form of capitalism, German entrepreneurs sought to break up the medieval inheritance and to accelerate the material recovery of their country. In 1835 the first German railroad was laid between Nürnberg and Fürth; by 1840 there were 282 miles of track; by 1850, 5,134 miles; and by 1860, over 6,600 miles. Locomotive factories were constructed in Essen, great steel plants in Solingen, textile factories in Silesia. In 1850 the Germanies produced only 208,000 tons of iron; by 1860 the output had risen to 1,391,555 tons. Agricultural experts, especially Albrecht Thaer and Justus Leibig, helped German agriculture make giant strides. The German postal system became one of the most efficient in the world.

Changes in the Social Structure. These remarkable economic changes were accompanied by shifts in the social order. The monarchies of the Confederation, in line with traditional practice, had rigidly excluded the middle class as well as workers and peasants from public life. But now the sudden spurt in industry and capitalism created antagonisms between the classes. The feudal aristocracy turned to large-scale agriculture and connecting industries. The new middle class was composed of businessmen, manufacturers, and professionals, who turned to both State and private employment. Opposed to these two classes was an essentially new proletariat, composed of landless peasants who had flocked to the towns after being dispossessed of their land.

The subsequent development of the class system was to play a vital role in German history. The nobility lost some of its privileges in 1848. Many of them turned to industry, where, together with the most successful middle-class capitalists, they formed a monied aristocracy, an oligarchy that was to control Prussia-Germany. The middle-class liberals either lost status or were forced out of the country by the events of 1848. Nineteenth-century Germany under Bismarck and William II was to have no responsible middle-class leadership and no firmly rooted peasantry.

The Zollverein. The economic position of the various German states after 1815 was aggravated by a bewildering variety of water, inland, and provincial tolls. Some 2,775 articles were subject to duties, which were collected by an army of 8,000 officials. In the German Confederation, 38 customs boundaries produced much the same effect as ligatures preventing the free circulation of blood. The merchant who traded between Hamburg and Austria, or Berlin and Switzerland, had to traverse ten states, be familiar with ten customs tariffs, and pay ten successive tariff dues. Prussia alone included regions with 67 different tariffs in the old provinces, with 119 different currencies.

The Zollverein developed gradually between 1818 and 1834, forged the bonds of economic unity that went hand-in-hand with political changes in the direction of national unification. The idea was orginally promulgated by Friedrich List (1789-1846), a Württemberger economist, but leadership in the Zollverein movement was gradually appropriated by Prussia. Prussia had little consideration for the welfare of other German states and no desire to see a customs union worked out by common consent. Instead, Prussian economic administrators began the process of economic amalgamation of their own territories, which lay scattered throughout the Germanies. Slowly but surely, economic pressure forced other German states one by one into the Prussian system. Both the South German and the Central German states, which desired customs unions of their own, were eventually drawn into the Prussian orbit. The Zollverein, announced on January 1, 1834, included 18 German states, in an area of 162,870 square miles and a population of more than 23 millions—all under Prussian leadership.

Friedrich List, the moving spirit in the formation of the Zollverein, was a battered and bruised soul during his lifetime, the target of unappreciative German industrialists and the prey of the Austrian secret police. His countrymen hurled such epithets at him as "revolutionary," "Jacobin," and "demagogue." To Metternich he was "an heroic swindler" and "the tool of squealing German manufacturers." After List's death, when it became obvious that his idea of national economy was in reality designed as a service to his country, he was placed on a pedestal as one of Germany's outstanding patriot heroes. He was now hailed as "a great German without Germany," "Germany's *verhinderte* Colbert," an economic genius who embodied the finest thinking of Cromwell, Canning, Dr. Quesnay, Robert Peel, even Aristotle. List was, indeed, a powerful factor in the unification of Germany. His concept of the Zollverein, his promotion of the German railway system, merchant marine, navy, and colonialism, and his themes of political economy—protective tariffs, Greater Germany, and *Mitteleuropa*—paved the way for Germany's political and industrial greatness. That List's ideal of a "practical, diligent, thrifty, enlightened, orderly, patriotic, and freedom-loving democracy" was not achieved in Germany may be attributed in part to the fact that subsequent

German political leaders confused national greatness with national aggression and utilized List's ideas as a basis for extremist thinking and policies.

— 6 —

THE REVOLUTION OF 1848

Disintegration of Metternich's System. The system of Metternich began to totter in 1830 after revolutions in France, Belgium, and Poland, with reverberations in the Germanies, where some of the minor princes felt themselves impelled to grant constitutions. At a meeting of some 25,000 persons at Hambach in the Palatinate in May 27, 1832, there were calls for a German union based on sovereignty of the people and for a European confederation of free republics. Metternich thereupon intensified his opposition to democrats and liberals. When, in 1848, another revolution began in France, it spread quickly to the Germanies, beginning in Baden and Württemberg and then running throughout the German states, until the whole country was aflame. In Prussia, Frederick William IV (1840-1861) promptly promised reform, but when assured of the support of the army, he crushed the rebellion. Metternich's system, however, had already collapsed, and its author fled ignominiously to England.

The Frankfort Assembly. The German liberals issued a call for a *Vorparlament* (Preliminary Parliament), which met and ordered general elections for a National Assembly to give Germany a constitution. The Frankfort Assembly convened on May 18, 1848, in St. Paul's Church in Frankfort-on-Main, established a provisional representative government, and chose the Archduke Johann of Austria as imperial regent. Several months later, the Assembly adopted a declaration of rights modeled on the

American Bill of Rights and the French Declaration of the Rights of Man. On the matter of the territorial problem the Assembly was hampered by the desires of the multinational Austrian monarchy and by the obvious Prussian urge to German leadership. Was there to be a "Big German" (*grossdeutsch*) solution, which would include the Germans of Austria, or a "Little German" (*kleindeutsch*) settlement, which would leave out the Austrian Germans in favor of Prussian hegemony? Once again the Germans were plagued by their old frustration of dualism. When the Prussian king was offered the crown of a united Germany by the Assembly, he refused to accept it on the ground that the offer "came from the gutter." As a convinced royalist, he would not accept "a dog-collar chaining him to the revolution." (*See Reading No. 12.*) The bitter inner dissensions, complicated by differences between conservatives, liberals, and radicals, were too much for the Assembly. Gradually, the disgruntled members withdrew, and a last-ditch rump parliament, meeting at Stuttgart, was dispersed by force.

Collapse of the Revolution. The once humiliated princes, now confident and able to stem the tide of revolt, turned viciously on the revolutionists. The liberals, especially, caught between the reviving autocracy and revolutionary radicalism, felt the wrath of the victors. Hundreds fled from the vengeance of the reactionaries. Heinrich Heine and Karl Marx remained in exile; Carl Schurz, Franz Sigel, and others emigrated to the United States, where they played an important role in the American Civil War; Richard Wagner and Theodor Mommsen returned reconciled to an authoritarian Germany. As the liberal gladiators retired from the political arena, the poet Ernst Moritz Arndt penned a remarkable prophecy:

> Away! Our heroes' arms grow tired,
> And stricken sore the strongest fall.
> A truce of life no more desired!
> Away! The death-knell tolls for all.

On February 4, 1850, the king of Prussia took the oath to a conservative constitution providing for a three-class system of voting that insured the political domination of the propertied stratum. The king retained an absolute veto on all legislation.

The Failure of 1848. Historians have ascribed various reasons for the failure of the Revolution of 1848 in the Germanies. Lewis B. Namier believes that the movement was unsuccessful because the great majority of the members of the Frankfort Assembly were not true liberals, but nationalists and imperialists. "The professorial lambs at Frankfort, bitten by the Pan-German dog, caught rabies." The Germans, Namier says further, managed to make other nations believe that there was something especially noble and liberal-minded about the collectivity of Germans at that time and about their performance—"one of the legends of history." To Peter Viereck, the Revolution was "a pathetic muddle": "The liberal university professors, Metternich's fiercest foes and now so prominent in 1848, were often far from the cloudy idealists pictured in our textbooks. . . . The majority . . . was more Bismarckian than Bismarck ever realized."

Koppel S. Pinson attributes the failure of the Revolution of 1848 in the Germanies to "the enormous disparity between the political aspirations of the German liberals and the mass support and actual power and influence they commanded." Eric Brandenburg lays the blame not on the Frankfort Assembly, but on "the power and self-assertion of the larger individual states, above all the two great powers [Austria and Prussia]." Edmond Vermeil sees the cause of failure not so much in external factors as in the mentality of the German people, molded and developed by peculiar German romanticism. German liberalism, he asserts, was extraordinarily weak, bowing before the work and will of pure power politics. A. J. P. Taylor considers it barren speculation to discuss the causes for the failure of the revolution: "There was no successful revolution in Germany; and therefore nothing to fail. There was merely a vacuum in which the liberals postured until the vacuum was filled." And Taylor again: "For the first time since 1521, the German people stepped on to the center of the German stage only to miss their cues once more. German history reached its turning point and failed to turn. That was the fateful essence of 1848."

Significance of the Revolution of 1848. The German Revolution of 1848 was something more than an ideological stage in German history. Intellectual ideas, indeed, provide one determinant of the course of history, but they must be considered in conjunction with other motivating factors. In his early career, Friedrich Meinecke explained the Revolution of 1848 in terms of pure idea. He was strongly criticized by Eric Brandenburg, who said: "I remain of the opinion that for the masses elemental experiences affecting and disturbing them in their daily, personal lives, are more powerful than doctrines and theories which are handed down to them from above. Only through the former are slumbering impulses and needs aroused or forced into the foreground of their consciousness."

1848 was, indeed, a tragic year in German history. On the surface, it seemed that the streams of rationalism —liberalism, democracy, social contract, egalitarianism, tolerance, constitutionalism—were converging in a common stream at last in the Germanies. For the first time in their history the German people seemed to have an opportunity to determine their own destiny. Critical decisions on German policy were for a time out of the hands of the autocratic princes and in possession of men who understood the currents of Western liberalism. German intellectuals suddenly found themselves the spokesmen for their people at a critical moment in their history. Predominantly middle-class (there was not a single working-class representative at Frankfort—the Assembly believed that nothing good could come from intrusion of the masses into politics) the intellectuals sought unity through persuasion, progress through moderation, and a better world through the practice of tolerance and goodwill. They failed.

When the wave of revolution receded, liberal nationalism was buried in the dregs, and the Prusso-German symbiosis was triumphant. Liberalism was submerged in the stronger movement of nationalism, and the people were left with a heritage of Prussian discipline, authority, and efficiency. The aim of the Revolution had been "through unity to freedom," but the events showed that unity was to be achieved through power. German unification was to depend from then on upon cohesion through force and force through cohesion. The new policy was *Eisen und Blut* as the strength went out of the liberal idea. For the rest of the nineteenth century and the first half of the twentieth, the ethical concept of liberty as a postulate of the human spirit fought a losing battle in Germany in both intellectual and political spheres. The tragedy affected not only Germany but the entire world.

— 7 —

BISMARCK'S WARS OF NATIONAL UNIFICATION, 1864-1871

Background: The Hegemony of Austria, 1849-1860. The failure of the Revolution of 1848 left the Germanics confused and divided again. Frederick William IV and his chief minister, Josef von Radowitz, recognizing the widespread desire for unity, proposed a friendly arrangement between Protestant Prussia and Catholic Austria, by which the two countries would control a common policy for all Germany. Radowitz organized the Erfurt Union, also called the Prussian Union, an association of princes under Prussia's protection, and urged that this smaller Bund be placed on an equal basis with the old Bund. Prince Schwarzenberg, the Austrian chancellor and successor to Metternich, strongly opposed the Prussian plan and insisted that only the Austrian sword could rule Germany. On September 1, 1850, Schwarzenberg officially announced the renewal of the old German Confederation.

There were now two German Bunds in existence, and the dispute soon turned into open conflict. The Elector of Hesse-Cassel, a member of the Erfurt Union, finding himself in constitutional difficulties with his parliament, called on the Frankfort Diet for assistance. When both confederations prepared to send troops into the country, war seemed inevitable. Schwarzenberg probably preferred an immediate settling of accounts with Prussia, but Francis Joseph was reluctant to make war on his fellow monarch. Frederick William, faced with insubordination by the jealous princes in his Union and uncertain of support by the reactionary Junkers, decided to retreat. When Tsar Nicholas, opposed to German unification of any kind, intervened in favor of Austria, the Prussian king gave up altogether. He dismissed Radowitz and sent Manteufel as successor to deal with the Austrians. By the Punctuation of Olmütz, signed on November 29, 1850, Prussia yielded, renounced the Erfurt Union, and recognized the revival of the German Confederation. Austria was once more in the saddle. To Prussian patriots the "humiliation of Olmütz" was a low point in their history; they resolved to seek revenge against Austria at the earliest opportunity.

The revived Confederation, striking immediately against liberalism and nationalism, renewed the old feudal and absolutist policies. Each German state competed with others in wiping out the vestiges of 1848. Despite her humiliation, Prussia in the 1850's began to emerge for the first time as an industrial power. Coal, iron, and steel poured in increasing quantities from the Ruhr valley; increasing urbanization of population went hand in hand with the development of the factory system; a network of new railways was constructed. The coronation of William I on October 16, 1861, gave hopes to depressed German nationalists who had been dissatisfied with the diplomatic confusion of Frederick William IV. In the meantime the Prussian General Staff, appalled by the failure of 1850, began to reorganize the Prussian army for another showdown with Austria. The new railways in Prussia were constructed carefully in conformity with a strategic plan worked out by the military leaders. Prussia was more than ever determined to make first a moral conquest of Germany and then dominate her by the sword.

Otto von Bismarck and German Unity. "I am a Junker and want to profit from it." These were the words of Otto von Bismarck (1815-1898), the outstanding political figure in the history not only of Germany but of the whole of Europe in the second half of the nineteenth century. Jules Favre, the French Foreign Minister in 1870, called him "a statesman who surpasses everything that I can imagine." A. J. P. Taylor terms Bismarck "the greatest of all political Germans, [who] assembled in his own person all the contradictions of German dualism." Erich Eyck attributes not only the unification of the German nation but also all the great landmarks of European history from 1860 to the First World War to Bismarck: "Everybody sees that; what is not so apparent, but not less important and far-reaching, is the transformation of the spirit and mentality of the German people, for which he is also responsible."

Aristocratic, conservative, militaristic, monarchistic, Lutheran in religion, Bismarck had no use for "phrasemaking and constitutions." He made it plain that he intended to secure by "iron and blood" what he believed could not be achieved by the honeyed words of liberals. (*See Reading No. 13.*) The reactionary genius of Europe, he defended all that was traditional in German history, including its feudal, monarchical features. A *Realpolitiker,* he was firmly convinced that Germany's destiny demanded guidance by the firm hands of the Hohenzollern dynasty. Originally a Pomeranian patriot, he soon saw that Prussia was destined for leadership in a united Germany; hence his local patriotism changed into a broader Prussian loyalty. Keeping only attainable ends in view, he led Prussia toward a new, powerful position. The man who once thought excusively in terms of Prussia soon welded the Germans into a united nation.

Bismarck's conception of the nation was a narrow one, more in line with the reason of state (*Staatsräson*) than other forms of the national idea. He was neither jingoistic, chauvinistic, nor racialistic nationalist, nor was he a totalitarian. Yet, as pointed out recently by Otto Pflanze, Bismarck fostered the tradition of the *Tatmensch,* the man of deeds who manipulates the reins of power and is responsible only to his conscience for the results. By synthesizing nationalism, autocracy, and militarism, Bismarck, perhaps unknowingly, contributed to the milieu out of which the Nazi movement emerged.

Nationalism meant to Bismarck that Germany was to be dominated by Prussia. He understood the dynastic loyalty of the various German peoples, but he believed that in order to be effective, German nationalism had to be dependent on the Hohenzollern dynasty. "Never," he said, "did I doubt that the key to German politics was to be found in princes and dynasties, not in publicists, whether in parliament and the press or on the barricades. The opinion of the cultivated public as uttered in parliament and the press might promote and sustain the determination of the dynasties, but perhaps provoked their resistance more frequently than it urged them forward in the direction of national unity. The weaker dynasties leaned for shelter upon the national cause; rulers and houses that felt themselves more capable of resistance mistrusted the movement. . . . The Prussian dynasty might anticipate that the hegemony in the future empire would eventually fall to it, with an increase of consideration and power." Nothing was to stand in the way of Prussia's drive to power. "If I have an enemy in my power," warned Bismarck, "I must destroy him." His permanent goal was to achieve a unified Germany, but this had to be attained along with two corollary aims: (1) the preservation of his own social class and (2) the destruction of the political philosophy of liberalism. "I am no democrat," he told Carl Schurz, "and cannot be one. I was born and raised an aristocrat."

In March, 1848, when the very existence of the Prussian monarchy was at stake, Bismarck, newly married and comfortably ensconced at Schönhausen, gathered fowling pieces, gunpowder, and peasants, and rushed off to offer his services to the king. Not only was he angry at the revolution, but he did not understand it. Bismarck began his political career on May 11, 1851, as Prussian representative to the Federal Diet at Frankfort. Although resurrected by Austria, the Bund was in reality moribund. Bismarck's mission to Frankfort opened a new epoch in German and European history. Certainly he planted the seeds of destruction in the Bund from the very first day he appeared at Frankfort. His stay there gave him a strong hatred and contempt for Austria and at the same time transformed him from a Prussian patriot into a German nationalist. As ambassador in St. Petersburg from 1859 to 1862 he became acquainted with one of the Great Powers that was to play an important role in his future policies. In 1862 he was Ambassador in Paris for a few months. Disraeli, who met him at this time, was deeply impressed by the blunt Junker: "Take care of that man," said the Englishman, "he means what he says."

Bismarck as Minister-President. Bismarck was forty-seven years old when he was named Minister-President of Prussia. His appointment came at a time when Prussia was undergoing one of the most crucial constitutional conflicts in her history. The new King of Prussia, William I, wanted to reorganize his military forces by increasing the power of the standing army at the expense of the militia. The House of Representatives refused to grant him the necessary funds, accusing him of desiring a large army "to stifle democracy." When the new Progressive party, opposed to the King, increased its representation in the elections of May 6, 1862, William seriously considered abdicating. In this crisis General Albrecht von Roon, Minister of War, prevailed upon the monarch to call Bismarck to Berlin. The fiery Prussian Junker was named Prime Minister and Minister for Foreign Affairs. Twenty-four years earlier, as a youth of twenty-three, Bismarck had said: "I want to make only that music which I myself like, or no music at all." Prussia, Germany, and the whole of Europe were to hear Bismarck's music for the next three decades.

Bismarck began his ministry by withdrawing the budget for the next year. Before a committee of the House he made a sensational speech describing his future course: it was essential, he said, that Germany should look not to liberalism but to her own power. The great questions of the day could not be solved by speeches and majority votes, he said further—that was the great mistake of 1848 and 1849—but by *iron and blood*. This was the policy that Bismarck was to pursue until the unification of Germany in 1871. His solution for the conflict between king and parliament was simple—he dissolved the assembly. From 1862 to 1866, he ruled arbitrarily without legislative consent, collecting funds and invigorating the military without sanction of the Chamber and the voters. So successful was he in his foreign policy during this period that the House, at its meeting in 1866, voted him a bill of indemnity legalizing all his acts during its absence.

Bismarck's course in his relations with Austria was clear: he was determined that Germany be unified under Prussian leadership, and that Austria be excluded from German affairs. He was blunt and direct in his warnings. He urged the Austrians to move the center of Hapsburg gravity eastward to Hungary, which would have meant the relinquishing of Austria's position in Germany. He held out an enticing bait—Prussia would become Austria's faithful ally if only she would do this.

War Against Denmark, 1864. Bismarck's first major step toward national unity was to use a quarrel with Denmark to test the powerful Prussian army and to mold a nationalistic public opinion. His great opportunity came with the death of King Frederick VII of Denmark on November 15, 1863. The question of Schleswig-Holstein had disturbed European diplomats for some time. Lord Palmerston has described the complicated problem in these words: "Only three men have ever understood it. One was Prince Albert, who is dead. The second was a German professor who became mad. I am the third and I have forgotten all about it." After the Treaty of Vienna in 1815, the two duchies of Schleswig and Holstein, both of which had large German populations, were united with Denmark in a personal union. Holstein was a part of the German Confederation, and the King of Denmark, as Duke of Holstein, was a member of the Confederation and was represented in the Diet at Frankfort. During the Revolution of 1848 the Germans in Schleswig and Holstein rebelled against the "Danish foreigners," but their insurrection collapsed when Prussian support was withdrawn.

From the beginning of his ministry Bismarck intended to annex the provinces to Prussia. "I have not the smallest doubt," he said, "that the Danish business can be settled in a way desirable for us only by war." All that was necessary was a favorable opportunity. It came in November, 1863, when the Danish Rigsraad passed a new constitution which Bismarck interpreted as incorporating Schleswig into Denmark and as a violation of the promise that the Danish king had given to Austria and Prussia in the Protocol of London in 1852. The death of Frederick VII brought the matter to a head.

Bismarck concluded an alliance with Austria, probably reasoning that he could eventually pick a quarrel with her over the spoils. On February 1, 1864, Prussian and Austrian armies crossed the frontiers of Schleswig. The Danes elected to fight, hoping desperately that England would come to their aid. Bismarck selected his moment shrewdly, for the British asked only that the integrity of the Danish monarchy not be violated. By April 18 the whole of Schleswig was in the hands of the invaders. Abandoned by the Great Powers, Denmark was forced to sue for peace. By the Peace of Vienna, August, 1864, Denmark had to give up the Duchies to Austria and Prussia. By the Convention of Gastein, August 14, 1865, the Austro-Prussian condominium of the Duchies was ended by dividing them. Austria was given control over Holstein and Prussia over Schleswig. The Austrians made the mistake of insisting that this partition be *provisional,* a shortsighted proposal that played directly into Bismarck's hands.

The result of the Danish war was received by Germans with tremendous jubilation. In the face of Austrian pretensions and the hostile Great Powers, Bismarck had engineered, boldly and almost recklessly, the most important territorial coup since the days of Frederick the Great. The victory gave Bismarck further ammunition in his continuing battle with parliament.

War Against Austria, 1866. Bismarck, who had never forgotten the humiliation at Olmütz and who never wavered in his intention to remove Austria as an obstacle to German unification, shrewdly isolated the Hapsburgs from foreign help. On April 8, 1866, he concluded an alliance with Italy, promising Venetia to the Italians in the event of a Prusso-Austrian war. This alliance was in direct defiance of the constitution of the German Confederation, which forbade any member to make an alliance with a foreign power against any other member. Living in dreams of Napoleonic splendor, Louis Napoleon was unable to adopt any hard and fast policy to thwart the designs of the scheming Prussian. Bismarck, on the other hand, was certain of his policy—he must goad Austria into aggression.

The issue again revolved around Schleswig-Holstein. On June 1, 1866, Austria challenged Prussia by submitting the question to the Federal Diet at Frankfort. On June 12 the Austrian ambassador at Berlin and the Prussian envoy at Vienna asked for their passports. When the Federal Diet passed an Austrian motion to mobilize the non-Prussian armies, Prussia declared the German Confederation ended and invited the German states to join a union under Prussian leadership. Bismarck now had his war with Austria. (*See Reading No. 15.*) "If we are beaten," he said, "I shall not return. I can die only once, and it befits the vanquished to die."

The superbly organized Prussian army demonstrated its superiority over the Austrians within a matter of seven weeks. On July 3, 1866, the Prussians inflicted a decisive defeat on the Austrians at Königgrätz (Sadowa). To the dismay of William I and the Prussian Junkers, Bismarck at once insisted upon moderate peace terms. The Treaty of Prague (1866) required Austria to recognize the end of the German Confederation, the incorporation of Schleswig-Holstein with Prussia, and the annexation of Venetia by Italy. Austria was to pay a small indemnity of twenty million talers, but she lost no territory. Bismarck, desiring Austrian neutrality in the event of a war with France, regarded these magnanimous terms as insurance for the future. "We shall need Austria's strength in the future for ourselves." Bismarck was now placed on a pedestal as the diplomatic genius of Prussia. Once again he had woven a victorious path through enormous difficulties, and had won a war against what had seemed to be insuperable odds.

There is still a difference of opinion among historians as to whether it was Bismarck's intention from the beginning to make war on Austria. There have been voluminous and not altogether convincing dissertations on both sides of the question. The conclusion of Erich Eyck: "Bismarck certainly never had any scruples about a war of this kind, which he himself in later years called 'fraternal.' But it is another question whether he *wanted* the war. The answer is that he would have been willing to do without the war if he had been able to achieve his aims by normal diplomatic means. It would have been out of harmony with his usual method if he had committed himself to war, even one day before he had made quite sure that no other way was open to him. . . . Although Bismarck was not from the beginning bent on war with Austria, he was engaged in a policy which made war unavoidable. The mistake of the Austrian statesmen was that they did not see in time that war was indeed inevitable, and that military and political preparations were necessary; but they cannot be reproached with having failed to avoid a war which was in no way avoidable." [1]

The North German Confederation, 1867. As a result of the Prussian triumph over Austria, the Prussian Hohenzollerns and not the Austrian Hapsburgs came to be the reigning dynasty in the German state. In 1867 Bismarck consolidated Prussia's position in the north by creating the North German Confederation, a union of twenty-two states and the principalities of North and Central Germany. A Reichstag was called on the basis of the universal suffrage law of 1849. The constitution of the confederation, written largely by Bismarck, was similar to the one adopted by the German Reich in 1871. It made the *Bundeskanzler* the responsible minister of the confederation and the political and administrative head of the government, which was precisely Bismarck's aim. There was a coating of democratic suffrage, but at the same time the people were deprived of real political power. This was in conformity with Bismarck's aim to kill parliamentarianism through parliament. Instead of a parliamentary government, Germany got a veiled absolutism. "Let us put Germany in the saddle," Bismarck said, "she will know how to ride."

The Indemnity Bill. Before embarking on the war against Austria, Bismarck had once again dissolved the House of Representatives. After the general elections of July 3, 1866, the new House was faced with the problem of indemnity for the government's infringements of the constitution. Bismarck introduced an indemnity bill to acknowledge that the illegal expenditures of recent years had to obtain a constitutional basis through subsequent vote. According to the bill, the House would approve the budgets of 1862-64, and the acts of the government during those years would not be considered unconstitutional. The bill was passed by a vote of 230 to 75, a complete triumph for Bismarck. (*See Reading No. 16.*) The strength of German parliamentary life ebbed away with ths decision. The irrepressible Bismarck, after the vote was announced, stated that he would repeat the same unconstitutional procedure if similar conditions rose

[1] Erich Eyck, *Bismarck and the German Empire* (London, 1950) pp. 125-26.

again. The shadow of 1862, when Bismarck showed his contempt for parliamentary institutions by ruling without parliament, hung over subsequent German constitutional development.

The Franco-Prussian War, 1870-71. · The final step in the creation of the Second German Reich was the Franco-Prussian War of 1870-71. Bismarck's brilliant successes of 1864 and 1866, together with the emergence of Italian nationalism, aroused the fears of Napoleon III. Aware that Germany and Italy as strong and unified national states would challenge French supremacy on the Continent, and determined to preserve the Napoleonic legend of military invincibility, Napoleon III tried at any cost to hinder the development of German unification. He had mixed feelings on the subject. In a speech from the throne on November 18, 1867, he said: "We must frankly accept the changes which have been introduced across the Rhine and let it be known that so long as our interests and our dignity are not threatened we shall not interfere with changes that have been evoked by the German nation." But to others he confided that, if Bismarck were to draw the South German states into the North German Confederation, "our [*the French*] guns will go off by themselves." Napoleon's confused diplomatic meddling gave Bismarck a chance to strike the final blow for German unity. Bismarck was not at all averse to a war with France, for he believed that the outbreak of conflict would swing the South German states into line, thereby completing German unification.

Using great diplomatic cunning, the Prussian isolated the Frenchman, making certain that Italy, Russia, Austria, and England would not assist Napoleon. The Prussian army, under General von Moltke, was in a high state of efficiency. Bismarck awaited his opportunity, which came with the conflict over the question of the projected Hohenzollern candidacy for the throne of Spain. In 1868 Queen Isabella of Spain was dethroned by a military coup. The monarchists, undoubtedly stimulated by Bismarck, proposed a candidate in the person of Prince Leopold von Hohenzollern-Sigmarin, a member of the Swabian branch of the Hohenzollern family. The specter of a revived empire of Charles V to threaten France on both sides of her borders was one to haunt the nervous French emperor.

When King William at Bad Ems was approached by Benedetti, the French ambassador, and was requested to abandon once and for all time any claims to the throne of Spain, the Prussian monarch immediately telegraphed an account of the meeting to Bismarck in Berlin. Unscrupulously editing the dispatch, Bismarck released it the next day, July 14, 1870. In abbreviated form, the telegram gave the impression of an ultimatum. Both the French and German people interpreted it as an unmitigated insult. (*See Reading No. 17.*)

France declared war immediately. The South German states, to Napoleon's utter consternation, joined Prussia. In less than two months the French armies were soundly defeated, and Napoleon was taken prisoner at Sedan. (*See Reading No. 18.*) After the siege and capitulation of Paris the war was terminated by the Treaty of Frankfort, May 10, 1871. (*See Reading No. 21.*) A humiliated France was required to cede Alsace and a part of Lorraine (including the fortresses of Metz and Didenhofen) to Prussia and to pay an indemnity of one billion dollars (five billion francs) within three years. Pending payment, the eastern departments of France were to be occupied. This time there was no generosity in the Prussian terms.

German unification was now completed, based on Bismarck's policy of iron and blood. The historian Heinrich von Sybel wrote passionately: "Tears run down my cheeks. By what have we deserved the grace of God, that we are allowed to live to see such great and mighty deeds. What for twenty years was the substance of all our wishes and efforts, is now fulfilled in such an immeasurably magnificent way." On January 18, 1871, King William of Prussia was proclaimed William I, German Emperor, at the Hall of Mirrors in Versailles. The North German Confederation was abolished, to be succeeded by the new German Empire consisting of Prussia and the North and South German states. (*See Reading No. 19.*)

Historians differ on the matter of responsibility for the outbreak of the Franco-Prussian War. Almost all German scholars insist that the war was forced on Bis-

by an envious France, and that he acted merely to
id the honor of the German nation. A. J. P. Taylor,
on the other hand, states that Bismarck deliberately provoked war with France over a trumped-up issue. Erich
Eyck is even more emphatic: "Responsibility for the war
rests in the first instance with Bismarck. He is, of course,
not the only person responsible. The unscrupulous French
journalists and politicians who frivolously cried: 'À
Berlin,' the Empress Eugénie, who influenced her hus-
band in favour of war, Napoleon himself and Gramont,
who threw away a splendid chance because they did not
know where to stop—they all have to bear their share of
responsibility. But they were all rather driven than driv-
ing. Bismarck alone kept the initiative by knowing beforehand how the others would react to his moves. He made
them his tools, and they did what he wanted them to do.
His superiority towers above them, head and shoulders.
Therefore, the primary responsibility rests with him
alone." [2] R. H. Lord distributes the responsibility to both
sides: "Unless one accepts the view that a Franco-Prussian war was under any circumstances inevitable, it is
difficult not to accuse both governments in 1870 of crim-
inally playing with fire."

— 8 —

THE ERA OF BISMARCK, 1871-1890

The New German Empire. The German Empire,
founded in January, 1871, was a federal union of twenty-
five states, each of which, though enjoying a measure of
local autonomy, was responsible to the central government at Berlin. The German Emperor, as president of
the federal union, was commander in chief of the army

[2] Eyck, *op. cit.*, pp. 173-74.

and navy; with the consent of the Bundesrat he could declare war and make peace. As King of Prussia, he exercised what amounted to dictatorial control over German affairs. The Bundesrat, representing the states, was composed of fifty-eight personal agents of the twenty-five states (Prussia, 17; Bavaria, 6; Saxony, 4; Württemberg, 4; Baden, 3; Hesse, 3; Mecklenburg-Schwerin, 2; Brunswick, 2; all others, 1 each). Since the representatives to the Bundesrat had to vote as a unit on instructions from their monarch, and since only 14 votes were enough to defeat any amendment to the constitution, Prussia, with her 17 votes, dominated the body. The Bundesrat had power to pass on all legislation, to accept treaties, to pass on the Emperor's dissolution of the Reichstag, and to confirm all appointments of federal officials. The Reichstag, elected by universal manhood suffrage, was a mere debating society. It could not initiate legislation nor overthrow the Chancellor. The Chancellor, appointed by the Emperor and responsible only to him, appointed administrative officials, directed foreign policy, and played an important part in shaping all legislation. (*See Reading No. 20.*)

The Role of Prussia. The Prussian Landtag (the legislative body of Prussia) was composed of two houses, the upper body consisting of the landed aristocracy and the lower body representing the property-holding bourgeoisie. The lower house was elected by a three-class system of voting—the electorate was divided into three groups according to the amount of taxes each voter paid. Each class elected one third of the members. As a result the small class of large taxpayers had as many votes as the considerably larger class of poor taxpayers. Even so, the Prussian Landtag had limited powers, and the German Emperor, as King of Prussia, exercised autocratic control. In practice the Prussian Prime Minister, who was at the same time the German Chancellor, became the real legislative power. Since the executive had no parliamentary responsibility, it was difficult if not impossible for the parliamentary leaders to represent the people.

Bismarck as Imperial Chancellor. The period of nearly twenty years from the foundation of the German Empire in January, 1871, to Bismarck's dismissal in March, 1890, is often called the Age of Bismarck. During this time he was the fulcrum not only of German but also of European politics. With a powerful army, an efficient bureaucracy, and a loyal bourgeoisie, Bismarck was able to prevent any revolutionary outbreaks. His domestic policy was to consolidate a powerful, centralized union under Prussian domination and to promote the prosperity of the new German Empire. As a means of maintaining German military supremacy he required all citizens to be conscripted for training. He proposed new civil and criminal laws, organized an imperial bank, unified the railroad system, and introduced a national system of coinage. Though at first a proponent of free trade, in 1879 he adopted a policy of protection for home industries. At first the only support Bismarck received in the Reichstag came from the National Liberal Party. To the left the Progressive Party cooperated in matters of unity, but in other matters was less willing to compromise with the government. The Center Party, formed in 1870, was designed to give political representation to Catholics. The Prussian conservatives rigidly opposed Bismarck on the ground that the events of 1866 and 1871 had diluted Prussian strength. The conservatives split into two groups, one of which, the Reich Party, for a time supported Bismarck. In general, however, Bismarck was firmly opposed to any internal rivals and insisted that all opposition to the Prussian conception of the state be crushed.

Bismarck's foreign policy was simple—to consolidate the position he had won for Germany. In the first period of his administration, from 1862 to 1871, he had waged three wars, enhanced Prussia, and unified Germany under the Prussian crown. Now Germany was *saturiert*. Bismarck regarded it as his vital task to maintain what Germany had acquired. He sought to solidify Germany's position in Europe by constructing a system of military alliances. Expecting France to seek revenge, he attempted to isolate her from any possible allies. In order to turn French eyes from the lost provinces of Alsace and Lorraine, he offered France a free hand "within reasonable limits" in North Africa. Meanwhile, he attempted to conciliate Britain by opposing German colonial expansion and discouraging the construction of a large navy.

The first step in the Bismarckian treaty system was

the Three Emperors' Conferences (1872-78) [William I of Germany, Francis Joseph of Austria, and Alexander II of Russia], which in effect restated the principles of the old Holy Alliance. When Russia's expansionist aims in the Balkans were checked at the Congress of Berlin (1878), Bismarck on October 7, 1879, negotiated the secret Austro-German Alliance, or Dual Alliance, directed against Russia. In 1881 Bismarck concluded the Three Emperors' League, which stated that if a fourth power attacked Germany, Austria, or Russia, the two remaining partners would maintain a benevolent neutrality. On May 20, 1882, Bismarck concluded the secret Triple Alliance of Germany, Austria-Hungary, and Italy, which provided that if any one or two of the allies were attacked by two enemy powers, the *casus foederis* would arise simultaneously for all the High Contracting Powers. For Germany the Triple Alliance meant a guarantee against French *revanche* as well as a means of extending her *Drang nach Osten* (drive to the east); for Austria, it was a bulwark against Russian expansion in the Balkans; and it was regarded by Italy as an aid in the conquest of Tunis and Tripoli in North Africa, as well as a means of counteracting French domination of the Mediterranean. In 1887 Bismarck, in order to "keep the wires to St. Petersburg open," negotiated the Reinsurance Treaty with Russia, by which he recognized Russian claims in the Balkans. This remarkable treaty system effectively maintained Germany's strong position on the Continent until the emergence of the Triple Entente (1907).

The Kulturkampf, 1871-1880. Bismarck was less successful in struggles on the domestic scene. No sooner was the Empire established than he embarked on a battle against what he described as "the enemies of the Empire." In 1864 Pope Pius IX had issued his *Syllabus of Modern Errors,* proclaiming civil marriage and secular education as "modern errors." In 1870 the Vatican Council announced that the Pope was "infallible" when speaking on matters of faith and morals. Both these proclamations angered Bismarck, but since he needed Catholic support at the time, he decided to await a more propitious moment to meet the "challenge." The struggle against the Catholic Church began in 1871. The Liberals, who joined the con-

flict, called it a "fight for civilization" (*Kulturkampf*);
Bismarck himself was concerned only with its political
aspects. He expelled the Jesuits from Germany in 1872
(*see Reading No. 22*) and promulgated the May Laws
(1872-1878) in the Prussian Landtag by which the state
was given complete control over marriage and education,
the Catholic press was muzzled, Church property was
confiscated, and recalcitrant priests, monks, and nuns
were persecuted. Archbishops, bishops, and priests were
deposed, imprisoned, and expelled. An inevitable result
was the rapid development of the Catholic Center Party
as a new and vital political power. Bismarck boasted that
he would not go to Canossa, as Henry IV had done in
1077, and submit to the papacy. But the concurrent rapid
growth of the Socialists in Germany convinced him that
the "red international" was considerably more dangerous
as an enemy of the Empire than the old "black international." The accession of the moderate Pope Leo XIII
(1878) facilitated Bismarck's change of heart. The
Chancellor abandoned the *Kulturkampf*. By 1887 virtually all the anti-Catholic laws were repealed, and Bismarck
sought clerical support in his battle against the Socialists.

   The Anti-Socialist Campaign, 1878-1890.   Bismarck
had only contempt for the Socialists, whom he regarded as
dangerous republicans, pacifists, internationalists, and
irreconcilable enemies of capitalism. In 1875 the Socialists, gathered at Gotha, united the followers of Ferdinand
Lassalle and Karl Marx. It was a warning Bismarck did
not intend to ignore. The number of Socialist voters had
risen from 124,000 in 1871 to 493,000 in 1877. When
two attempts were made on the life of the Emperor in
May and June, 1878, Bismarck had his pretext for striking a blow against the hated enemy, despite the fact that
neither of the assassins was a member of the Socialist
Party. In 1878 Bismarck had the Reichstag enact a series
of Exceptional Laws forbidding freedom of the press and
initiating a campaign of persecution against "the socialist
machinations dangerous to the common weal." (*See Reading No. 23.*) These measures were explicitly directed
against the Socialists, but it was apparent that Bismarck
in a subtle way was also directing his fire against the
Liberals. At the same time Bismarck inaugurated a series

of social reforms designed "to take the wind out of the sails of the Socialists." He asked the Reichstag "to heal social evils by means of legislation based on the moral foundations of Christianity." A number of social reforms was passed: sickness insurance (1883), accident insurance (1884), and old age insurance (1889). The working class was not appeased by these concessions, which it regarded as a politically inspired conciliatory bribe.

Once again, repression proved to be a stimulus to revolutionary agitation. The Socialists went underground, and despite all efforts to eliminate them as a political factor, they thrived and grew in numbers. The Exceptional Laws, originally enacted for 2½ years and thereafter renewed, were allowed to expire in 1890, the year of Bismarck's retirement.

— 9 —

ECONOMIC, SOCIAL, AND INTELLECTUAL CURRENTS, 1870-1914

Germany in the New Industrial Revolution. The economic transformation of Germany in the second half of the nineteenth century from a predominantly agrarian to a modern industrialized nation is one of the most striking and spectacular phenomena of European history. (*See Reading No. 14.*) Several factors were responsible for the remarkable rapidity and magnitude of German economic expansion. With the achievement of national unification in 1871, Germany plunged wholeheartedly into the New Industrial Revolution. Her strategic position in Central Europe now made her logically the leader of Continental trade, and her great coastal cities, especially

Bremen and Hamburg, were excellent ports of entry. A late start in industrialization gave her an additional advantage in that her industries could be equipped from the outset with the most modern machinery. Thoroughness in research and skill and discipline in production and distribution enabled Germany to take a place as one of the world's great industrial nations and to challenge British and American supremacy in the markets of the world. The speed of Germany's economic development nearly equaled that of the United States.

Increase in Population.   Along with industrialization occurred a radical change in population, both in numbers and distribution. At the opening of the nineteenth century the area of Germany later equivalent to the Bismarckian Reich housed a population of about 24 millions. By 1914, despite an annual average of some 70,000 emigrants, the population of Wilhelmian Germany had risen to 67,790,000 with a density of population of about 125 inhabitants per square kilometer. To some extent this extraordinary increase may be attributed to a falling death rate, innovations in modern medicine, and sanitary improvements. There was a rapid shift of population from the rural areas to the towns and cities. In 1850 only 2.8 per cent of the population lived in cities of more than 100,000 population; by 1910 this percentage had increased tenfold. Berlin, which in 1820 had only 200,000 inhabitants, had a population of 2,071,907 in 1910—the fifth largest city in the world.

Industrial Expansion.   German industrial expansion during the late decades of the nineteenth century and the early twentieth century presents an imposing picture. Of special significance was the expansion of the state-controlled railway lines: in 1860 there were 11,026 kilometers of railway tracks in Germany; in 1910 they had increased to 59,031 kilometers. German coal production, which centered chiefly in the Ruhr and the Saar regions, increased from 29,398,000 metric tons in 1871 to 191,500,000 in 1913; Germany thus became the great producer of coal after the United States and Britain. From the early 1880's onward, Britain gradually lost the industrial leadership she had enjoyed during most of the century, as indicated by the following comparative table of iron extraction:

IRON EXTRACTION

(*in tons*)

Year	Great Britain	Germany
1850	2,300,000	350,000
1900	8,959,691	8,381,373
1902	8,839,124	17,586,521

The German iron and steel industries expanded rapidly. During the period from 1882 to 1892, German exports of iron and steel rose by 11 per cent, while English exports of the same products dropped by 37 per cent. Huge iron and steel empires were created by the Krupps, Thyssens, and Stumm-Halbergs.

Germany also became Britain's rival in shipping. Germany's tonnage was steadily augmented until by 1913 her merchant marine, which consisted almost entirely of new vessels using steam, reached a net tonnage of more than three million. Two great shipping companies, the Hamburg-American Line and the North German Lloyd of Bremen, formed one of the most powerful merchant fleets in the world. German agents established business connections in all continents.

The United States had originated the idea of mass production in the New Industrial Revolution; Germany's special contribution was innovation in the chemical industry. German scientists took good advantage of the rich salt and potash beds in Saxony, Thuringia, and Alsace. The most remarkable development was in synthetic dyes, drugs, and *ersatz* (substitute) rubber, oil, and nitrates. German scientific leadership in organic chemistry was of extraordinary importance in World War I: when Germany was cut off from South American supplies of nitrates for use in explosives, Professor Fritz Haber developed a process of extracting nitrates from air, an epoch-making discovery that enabled Germany to hold out in the conflict for four years.

Another important factor in German economic prosperity was the great development of the electrical industry. At the opening of the twentieth century Germany was using a greater variety of electrical products than any other country in the world. Two giant firms—Siemens and Halske, directed by Werner von Siemens, and the Allgemeine Elektrizitäts Gesellschaft (AEG), directed by Emil Rathenau—competed with each other in constructing power transmission systems and a network of electric railways.

The Armaments Industry. The armaments industry in Germany was regarded not only as one of the major causes for industrial prosperity but also as an indispensable corollary of national interests. During the Franco-Prussian War of 1870-71 the Krupp works at Essen supplied the Prussian army with highly effective artillery. The world-wide reputation of Krupp armaments brought orders to Essen from all continents; this foreign demand added to that of the German military machine resulted in a tremendous increase in Krupp business. German performance in the armaments industry was a powerful factor in the snowballing arms race that preceded World War I.

Banking and Industrial Concentration. Germany's rapid industrial and commercial expansion was eased by a banking system that was geared closely to the promotion of economic life. The new German banks worked closely with industrial corporations, providing huge credits for expansion and participating directly in management. This procedure ran directly counter to British experience, for British banks were not able to meet the tremendous demands of the new industries. So successful was the German practice that by the end of the nineteenth century Germany's strong banking system was exporting capital along with industrial enterprise.

One of the major results of large-scale industrialism in Germany was the trend toward huge enterprises, called cartels, which were used to protect invested capital, eliminate competition, stabilize profits, and avoid business cycles. There were different types of cartels—to fix prices, limit production or supply, centralize certain markets, or regulate foreign trade—but in all cases the tendency was characteristically monopolistic. There were some disadvantages: small industry was submerged or kept at a disadvantage, prices were maintained at a high level, and the mercantile classes were reduced to little more than figureheads. But from the German point of view this was a small price to pay to escape from the economic anarchy characteristic of those countries where cartels had not been developed.

The Interessen Gemeinschaft der Farben Industries, commonly called I. G. Farben, emerged in the twentieth century as the world's most powerful industrial combination. It controlled more than 380 firms scattered over Germany, along with some 500 enterprises in foreign countries, in a closely interlocking relationship. Party to 2,000 cartel agreements, it manufactured 43 major products, which it distributed throughout the world. It had at its command an army of scientists, industrialists, statesmen, even spies. A huge economic octopus, it used its restrictive power of patent tie-ups with industrialists of foreign nations to slow up production of strategic war materials in countries that the Germans considered potential enemies. After World War II, 24 leading officers of I. G. Farben were brought to trial at Nuremberg for "wilfully engaging in activities indispensable to Germany's aggressive warfare," the first such indictment of businessmen in history.

Education for Industry. Germany's industrial battles were won in her institutes of technology, trade schools, and industrial continuation schools. The emergence and development of these scientific and technical institutions after 1871 played an important part in Germany's rise as an industrial power. The *technische Hochschulen,* or polytechnic schools and institutes of technology, modeled on the French *école polytechnique,* were oriented in the interests of higher science, with special attention to practical uses of electricity, motors and machinery, ship-building, construction of all kinds, and the application of science to chemistry. Special commercial institutes, called *Handelshochschulen,* supported by the city governments or by the chambers of commerce, were devoted to scientific investigation of production and consumption in the world's markets. Of university caliber, these schools sent a stream of experts into commerce and the state service. Trade schools, called *Fachschulen,* financed by the state, specialized in different occupations such as building, machine-making, metal work, and weaving. The most important educational institutions in industrial training were the *Fortbildungsschule,* or continuation schools, some compulsory and some voluntary. The purpose of these schools was to get the children after they had left elementary school and train them as citizens and workers. In Prussia in 1912 there were 2,637 continuation schools, with 455,-478 scholars.

Behind this thorough organization of industrial schools was a deliberate campaign to capture the markets of the world in the increasing economic struggle between the Great Powers. No stone was left unturned to help the nation forge ahead. Ernest F. Henderson describes a continuation school at Frankfort-on-Main in these words:

> In all the classes the difference between good and bad materials is insisted upon, and it is shown that a reputation for integrity will outweigh any slight momentary increase in profits. The pupils are taught very carefully to compute the cost of each item, including every minute of their own labor, and then to add only a reasonable and normal profit. Such ideas, thus spread throughout the empire, have very quickly raised the whole level of industry and paved the way for world conquest.[1]

From Laissez Faire to Protection. Until the late 1870's the economic policy of Germany was moderate *laissez faire*. The interests of the landed classes were identical with those of the free traders, and the growth of population kept the country prosperous despite free trade. Up to this time Germany was exporting more grain than she was importing. The building of railways in both the United States and Russia resulted in the competition of cheap grain. Bismarck was converted to a policy of protection in agriculture for several reasons: he did not want to see his country transformed into a purely industrial nation; he believed that a flourishing agriculture was necessary for self-sufficiency in war, a strong rural life was necessary to preserve traditional conservativism, and tariff duties would provide a new source of revenue.

Protection of iron was just as important as protection of grain. After the financial panic of 1873 the German iron and steel industrialists for the first time began demanding a protective tariff, on the ground that free trade and liberalism had resulted in German markets being flooded by manufactures from England and France. When the elections of 1878 brought a protectionist majority, the Reichstag on June 12, 1879, by a vote of 217 to 117

[1] Ernest F. Henderson, *A Short History of Germany* (New York, 1917) pp. 538-39.

passed a protective tariff. Protectionism was in effect an important step in the creation of a powerful Greater Germany. Politically, it represented another blow to liberalism, democracy, and constitutionalism by the agrarian and industrial interests combined with the crown.

German Colonialism. Closely associated with the rising industrialization was the emergence of German colonialism. Before 1871 Bismarck had neither thoughts of nor the possibility of acquiring colonies for Germany; from 1871 to 1881 he adopted a course of watchful waiting for the desired opportunity; after 1881 he inaugurated a cautious but definite colonial policy. His attitude in 1871 was expressed in a typical Bismarckian aphorism: "A colonial policy for us would be like the silken sables of Polish families who have no shirts." In conformity with the then current anti-imperialist *Zeitgeist*, he looked upon colonies only as a means of providing sinecures for officials and he concluded that they were too costly a luxury for Germany. In the middle 1870's he regarded as obstacles to a German colonial policy the *Kulturkampf*, the jealousy of France, the acute irritability of England, and Germany's own unconfident position in world affairs. But in the 1880's the *Kulturkampf* was at an end, the *revanche* policy of France had been softened, and Germany's position in Europe had been strengthened in 1882 by the Triple Alliance. Impatient at British delays and knowing that he held trump cards, he assumed a bullying attitude and successfully inaugurated the creation of a colonial empire by taking Angra Pequena in South-West Africa.

Germany had all the motivating factors for colonial expansion—need for raw materials, for food supplies, and for outlets for capital. A late starter in the Africa hunt, she, nevertheless, obtained several areas: the Cameroons, Togoland, German South-West Africa, and German East Africa. Although large in size, her share of Africa was comparatively poor in natural resources. Later, she was checked in North Africa by Britain and France, in the Balkans by Russia, and in the Near East and Far East by Britain and other powers. On June 1, 1914, William II sent a message to President Wilson complaining that "all the nations of the world are directing the points of their bayonets at Germany."

Social Consequences of the Industrial Age. The rapid industrialization of Germany brought with it all the social problems generally associated with the industrial age. But where social reform was slow and painful in England and the United States, it was almost immediate in Germany. A highly organized system of social legislation was introduced by Bismarck, starting in 1881, with a thoroughness that aroused the interest and even admiration of the entire world. Germany was a welfare state even before World War I. The implementation of this system was due in large part to the fact that the tradition of paternalism worked to destroy the resistance of those who opposed social reform. Bismarck was certain that social reform was the business of the state, not of the Socialists.

After Bismarck's anti-Socialist legislation, Socialist organization increased by leaps and bounds. There was a tremendous growth of membership in the trade unions, despite strong opposition by the heavy industrialists.

The Nature of German Nationalism. There was scarcely any feeling of national consciousness in the Germanies of the late eighteenth century. Goethe, the cosmopolitan, regarded "all national poetry as hackneyed or would become so, if it is not based upon what is universally human." Neither German intellectuals, nobles, nor peasants saw any need to unify some three hundred kingdoms, duchies, counties, and free cities into a compact national state in which national sentiment would transcend traditional local loyalties. The waves of the French Revolution—liberty, equality, and fraternity—passed over the Germanies with scarcely any impression. Most Germans were alienated by what they called the excesses on the other side of the Rhine. But the impact of the Napoleonic conquest was decisive. The attempt of the Corsican to spread the ideals of the French Revolution, as interpreted by himself, into the Germanies by force of arms provided the exterior spark which ignited the fires of German nationalism.

From this point on, the building of German nationalism was as artificial as the construction of the Panama Canal. Prussia had gradually developed into the strongest German state, and from her came the initiative and drive for liberation from Napoleon. "In the north breaks the dawn of freedom," sang Körner, who, along with many others, enrolled in the volunteer Prussian corps. The uprising soon assumed a national character, but it still remained Prussian to the core. Such is the irony of history —the impetus for German nationalism came not from the heart of the German states most concerned, but from the outside—from a relatively crude, backward border state which by force of events was able to superimpose its own system on Germany.

German nationalism was the offspring of a fusion of Prussianism and romanticism, which in many ways were direct opposites. Peter Viereck sees an important psychological implication here: "Germans accepted authoritarian Prussianism so enthusiastically precisely because it was so un-German. They accepted it as the opposite extreme, the needed overcompensation, of what they unconsciously sensed as their most dangerous and most typical quality: their intoxication with chaos, their anarchic Faustian romanticism."

German nationalism quickly took on an illiberal character. Instead of merging in a common pattern, Western and German thought veered off in different directions. In the Anglo-Saxon-French-American world, the concept of individual liberty and rational cosmopolitanism appeared in the eighteenth-century Enlightenment. A pluralistic and open society emerged out of a struggle by the people for freedom, constitutionalism, tolerance, and a free society based on natural law. Originally influenced by the Western Age of Reason, the educated classes in Germany gradually turned away from the "alien" rationalism and liberalism of the West. German intellectual thought (Hegel, Treitschke, *et al.*) gradually accepted the virtues of an authoritarian, closed society with emphasis upon the state instead of the people, the precivilized folk concept instead of rationalism, the ideal fatherland with a mission instead of a belief in political integration round a rational goal.

It was the tragedy of her history that Germany was caught in this fatal dichotomy between Western rationalism and Eastern authoritarianism and was unable to resolve the unending intellectual conflict. Again and again there appeared in German intellectual circles scholars who well understood the implications of Western intellectual concepts. But again and again in Germany the political reality centered around thinkers and activists who emphasized xenophobic nationalism, worship of the state, peculiarities of race or class, and narrow, antagonistic historicism. Germany and the West went separate ways.

Early Apostles of German Nationalism. The first major proponents of German nationalism appeared in the darkness of Napoleonic despotism. Friedrich Ludwig Jahn (1778-1852), an eccentric demagogue deeply moved by the humiliation of his people, devoted his life to the cause of German nationalism. Conceiving the idea of reviving the morale of his countrymen by improving their physical condition through the practice of gymnastics, he borrowed the basic elements of Swedish drill and set up a series of gymnastic exercises designed to develop the physical and moral powers of German youth. He called for a self-assertive, self-confident nation, which, far from taking the orders of a foreign conqueror, would be ready to take a leading position in world society. Turnvater Jahn's *magnum opus, Das deutsche Volkstum* (1810), was a kind of handbook of nationalism designed to lead the German people to an understanding and appreciation and love of the Fatherland. Written with almost religious intensity, it became, according to German critics, "one of the most German of all books" and "one of the most precious products of the German Spirit."

The Grimm brothers, Jakob Ludwig Karl (1785-1863) and Wilhelm Karl (1786-1859), the founders of scientific Germanistics, were among a small group of dedicated men who fashioned a popular national German literature. From the outset they took the romantic position that was closely allied with the rising German nationalism. In the same manner as the early romantics—the Schlegel brothers, Tieck, Novalis, Herder, Fichte, Schelling, and Schleiermacher—the Grimms in their philological investigations sought to unlock the poetry and the experiences of the German people which were encased in words and grammatical forms. Like the romantics, the Grimms issued a plea for the imagination, for emotion and feeling, for individualism, and above all, for a synthetic expression of the national genius in all its manifold aspects of literature, art, religion, and philosophy.

Nationalism in German Historiography. The beginnings of nationalist German historiography may be traced to the writings of Justus Möser (1720-1794), a comparatively obscure publicist and statesman, who was posthumously granted the veneration accorded the early prophets of German nationalism. Whereas Möser, the small-town official, saw the salvation of the German nation in its healthy, small rural freeholders, the poet, philosopher, theologian, and historian Johann Gottfried von Herder (1744-1803) painted the German nationality on the much broader canvas of universal history. As an humanitarian nationalist, Herder advocated a spirit of tolerance and regard for the rights of other nationalities. His most important influence on the development of nationalism was made in his erroneous teaching of the permanence of national character.

From Herder to Hegel, German historical writing became obscured in the shadows of romanticism and in the theology of the transcendental idealists. Georg Wilhelm Hegel (1770-1831), generally regarded as one of the leading apostles of German nationalism, was, in the words of H. C. Engelbrecht, "the magician who sought to unify the romantic theories of the *Volksgeist* and the unknown organic development with historical reality and the diversity of historical life." With all the honorific phrases at his disposal Hegel praised the omnipotent State, beside which the fate and happiness of the individual counts for nothing. As the *praeceptor Borussiae,* Hegel shaped and stamped German political thought and development from his time on. For decades, Hegelian disciples occupied most of the chairs of philosophy, history, and political economy at Prussian universities. Many generations of schoolmasters were grounded in the doctrines of Hegelianism, which they in turn imparted to hosts of school children. In Hegel they found pontifical authority for the thesis that Prussian authoritarianism was good, desirable, and inevitable. Prusso-Germany was molded in the Hegelian image.

Parallel to the emergence of Prussia as the dominant political power in the Germanies was the appearance of the Prussian school of historiography. Friedrich Christoph Dahlmann (1785-1860), Johann Gustav Droysen (1808-1884), Heinrich von Sybel (1817-1895), and Heinrich von Treitschke (1834-1896) all believed that the writing of history should be made subservient to the needs of the Prussian state. Treitschke, for example, glorified the State, the hero, and power and denounced "rationalistic liberalism, unpatriotic social democracy, money-grubbing Britain, and disintegrating Judaism." He advocated war as a national necessity: "War is elevating, because the individual disappears before the great conception of the State." (*See Reading No. 24.*)

German Irrationalism. Some of the greatest and most fruitful philosophic thought has come from Germany. The intellectual history of the world has been enriched immeasurably by the contributions of Leibniz, Kant, Goethe, the post-Kantian idealists, and the logical positivists. At the same time, there were irrationalist elements in German pseudo-philosophy that achieved significance because of the political use to which they were put. The predilection of the German intelligentsia for abstract subjectivism strongly affected the entire range of German culture and education. Steeped in mysticism and devoid of common sense and self-criticism, these pseudo-philosophers descended to absurdities and an emotionally destructive irrationalism.

The new type of pseudo-scholarship began with Julius Langbehn (1851-1907), who, in his *Rembrandtdeutsche* (1890), claimed that Germany had become immobilized in the quagmire of reason and knowledge. He insisted that intuition was higher than knowledge. Two foreign writers, Arthur de Gobineau (1816-1822), a Frenchman, and Houston Stewart Chamberlain (1855-1927), an Englishman, both of whom sang praises to the cultural superiority of the Aryan "race," enjoyed tremendous success in Germany. Gobineau held that all human races are unequal, that there is no true civilization among the European peoples where the Aryan branch is not prominent, and that the whole course of human history can be explained by the degeneration of "noble races" by mixture with inferior blood. Chamberlain, who became a naturalized German, attempted to present "scientific" proof that history and character intersected in the innately superior Teutonic "race" (in which he included Christ, Dante, Shakespeare, Goethe, and Kant).

This tradition of irrationalism, mysticism, and intuition was further stimulated by the prose works of Richard

Wagner (1813-1883), the great composer, who set his neo-romanticism in the framework of a mechano-materialistic world, and added to it the worship of the *Fuehrer-State* and the nonsensical doctrines of race. "What is the German thing?" asked Wagner. "This must also be the right thing." With Wagner the accent on the German Folk-Spirit as the true test of freedom reached the proportions of a mania. The Jews were un-German, he said, the press was un-German, democracy was un-German. According to Paul Henry Lang, "there has seldom been a human life presenting such an artistic web of conscious untruth and self-deceiving, pathetic world-conceit. . . . By mixing new charm potions in the German mental vapors Wagner contrived as much if not more to the rising superiority of the Second Reich as Bismarck."

German irrationalism carried over into the twentieth century in the works of Oswald Spengler (1880-1936) and Alfred Rosenberg (1893-1946). Spengler's masterpiece, *The Decline of the West,* bristling with ponderous documentation, was an esoteric *tour de force* devoted to such mystic ideas as "cosmic force," "race beauty," and "voice of the blood." Alfred Rosenberg, the official Nazi philosopher, sought to give a "scientific" justification for the prevailing Nazi blood myth. What was left of German humanism and rationalism was dissolved in a confused neo-romanticism, spurious and undignified. German society was corroded and perverted by these thinkers who preached fanatical nationalism, infantile mysticism, worship of power, and hostility to liberalism, democracy, and humanitarianism.

Militarism. Militarism infected all countries in varying degrees. But there arose especially among Prusso-German intellectuals an enthusiasm for war itself as an ennobling experience. Heinrich von Treitschke recognized the Prussian army as "the embodiment of national characteristics and virtues," and extolled the proud military instinct of the army as "an indispensable blessing." Bismarck was certain that "it is not the wolf's fault that God created him the way he was." Education was reformed as an adjunct to the military machine, on the assumption that "national school-time keeps body and soul together in strength and vigor." The military way of life penetrated into government, bureaucracy, and

business. It conditioned the mass of the German population, which became convinced that Germany could reach
the level of national and world power only through the
might of the sword. Significantly, even so levelheaded an
intellectual as Thomas Mann (who later revised his
beliefs) was swept away by the military spirit in 1914:
"German militarism is the manifestation of German
morality. . . . The militarism inherent in the German
soul, its ethical conservatism, its soldier-like morality—
an element of daemonism and heroism: this is what refuses to recognize the civilian spirit as a final ideal of
mankind." (*See Readings Nos. 29, 30, and 32.*)

The Great General Staff.   Closely allied with German militarism was the expert professional leadership of
the Prussian—and later the German—Great General Staff.
With the beginning of the industrial age, war was taken
out of the hands of monarchs and aristocrats and was
directed by highly specialized, anonymous technicians.
The General Staff developed a set of rigid traditions:
anonymity in planning and command, complete divorcement of military from political affairs, strict moral and
intellectual standards, and an inflexible caste system.
The German method of staff organization was considered
so excellent that it was used as a model by the military
leaders of nearly every great power as well as many
small ones.

Germany's system of military organization was led by
a succession of officer-aristocrats: Scharnhorst, Boyen,
Gneisenau, Clausewitz, the two Moltkes, Waldersee,
Schlieffen, Hindenburg, Ludendorff, Seeckt, Schleicher,
Beck, Keitel, and Jodl. The General Staff was not destroyed by the Treaty of Varsailles, although its leadership of German militarism was known by the Allied
authorities; it merely changed its name and carried on
as the *Truppenamt* under the office of the *Herresleitung*.
During the era of National Socialism, the General Staff
was torn between its ethical and patriotic responsibilities
on the one side and by the military oath on the other.
Hitler, who was completely convinced of his own military genius and brooked no rivalry inside Germany,
smashed the General Staff and set up his own *Oberkom-
mando Wehrmacht* (OKW) under Keitel with its Nazi-
loyal staff under Jodl.

Military experts claim that the long history of the General Staff in Germany was to some extent responsible for the aggravation of an expansionist, adventurous, and militaristic national temperament. Despite its insistence upon an almost monkish divorcement of military policy from political affairs, the General Staff has functioned as a powerful factor in the historical development of Germany in the last several centuries. It provided a deadly effective leadership in the German drives for world power in the twentieth century. Its influence was not merely national; it had an effect upon military thinking and political decisions throughout the entire world.

Nationalistic Societies.   German nationalism was further stimulated by the rise of nationalistic societies, organizations devoted to the furtherance of national aspirations. The German Naval Society called for a huge navy, thereby arousing the resentment of Englishmen, who had long regarded the waves as being ruled by the British fleet. The German Colonial Society issued propaganda calling for the acquisition of colonies, even though Germany had been late on the scene in the spoliation of Africa and the Far East. The East Mark Association energetically demanded Germanization of the Poles, while other nationalistic societies called for the Germanization of Alsace-Lorraine and other areas of dispute. Associations, notably the Pan-German League, were formed for the preservation of *Deutschtum* in foreign lands. On the domestic scene nationalistic societies encouraged the use of the German language, German sports, and German national education. These organizations, sponsoring patriotism and fostering the "serve Germanism" ideal, gave direction and power to the new German nationalism. There were similar societies in all nations, but in Germany they were especially active and influential.

Germany and Democratic Institutions.   Among historians there has been a strong difference of opinion on the extent of democratic development in Germany. One group holds that despite the persistence in German history of authoritarianism in one form or another, from Prussian autocracy to the plebiscitarian Caesarism of the Weimar Republic, there is a sound basis for representative government. These historians say that there is plenty of evidence to show that the democratic idea is perfectly familiar to the German people. Another group of historians believe that it is questionable whether the German people or their rulers, on the basis of their historical experience, have been deeply attracted by the possibility of a long-term and peaceful evolution of political democracy. Again and again in German history, they say, constitutional "development" was achieved not by peoples conquering their rulers, as had been the case in Britain, France, and the United States, but rather as the more or less free gift of rulers who made concessions as a result of military defeat and national humiliation. From the pseudoparliamentarianism of the Kaiserreich to the Nazi Third Reich the fulcrum of political power has consistently remained at the upper levels, where parliamentarianism was held in contempt. Frederick the Great called the Reichstag "a phantom, an assembly of publicists . . . who bark at the moon like watchdogs." In 1837 Ernst Augustus, King of Hanover, in abrogating the constitution of 1832, announced that "professors, prostitutes, and ballet dancers can be had anywhere for money." Frederick William I proclaimed: "I leave the stink of the Diet to my gentlemen Junkers." Frederick William IV refused to accept "a crown of filth and mud from the hands of the people's representatives." Albrecht von Roon, Bismarck's sponsor, spoke of "the constitutional swindle" and the "cesspool of liberalism," while Bismarck himself loathed "the muddy wave of parliamentarianism" and denounced it in his famous "iron and blood" speech. William II was certain that "there is only one master in this country," prompting the historian Mommsen to complain about "the pseudo-constitutional absolutism under which we live." To Hitler democracy was simply "a putrescent corpse."

WILHELMIAN GERMANY, 1888-1918

The Ninety-Nine Days of Frederick III. Emperor William I, who had passed the age of ninety, died in March, 1888. His son, the Crown Prince, ascended the throne as Frederick III at the age of fifty-six. Unfortunately, this tragic figure of the Hohenzollern dynasty was suffering from a fatal disease, cancer of the throat; his reign lasted just ninety-nine days. Frederick III who was married to the eldest daughter of Queen Victoria of England, had been deeply impressed by British constitutional institutions. But the great hope of German liberals died with him.

William II (1888-1918). Frederick III's son and successor, William II (1888-1918), who ascended the throne at the age of twenty-nine, presented a sharp contrast to his liberal father. The young emperor was an extraordinary individual, whose character embraced a world of contradictions. Though intelligent, talented, and cultivated, he was inclined to act at times in a highly erratic manner. On occasion, he could be a most engaging person, but he could easily change into an impatient, fickle, and clumsy boor. Although aware of the responsibilities of his position, he was nevertheless susceptible to the flattery of courtiers. Both as prince and ruler he endeavored to study all the problems of business, art, science, and government. Possessing a remarkable memory and the willingness to learn, he surrounded himself with leading scholars, industrialists, and artists. At the same time, his nature was so impulsive that he scarcely penetrated deeply into any of the problems he studied and almost invariably gained only superficial impressions.

A sincere patriot, William II was convinced beyond the

shadow of a doubt that his high position was entrusted to him by God. He firmly believed it to be his duty to maintain the monarchy that had been bestowed on him by divine Providence. "I regard my whole position," he said, "as given to me direct from heaven and I have been called by the Highest to do his work; by One to whom I must one day render an account." In another speech he proclaimed: "Remember that the German people are chosen by God. On me, as the German Emperor, the spirit of God has descended. I am His weapon, His sword, His vice-Regent." To his friend "Nicky" (Nicholas II, Tsar of Russia) he wrote: "A sacred duty is imposed by Heaven on us Christian Kings and Emperors—to uphold the doctrine of the Divine Right of Kings." (*See Reading No. 31.*)

William II's nationalistic, bombastic, and warlike utterances were probably compensatory gestures for what was in reality a weak, uncertain personality. On April 24, 1891, he told the students at Bonn University: "You must be glad in your hearts at being young Germans, and when you stroll along the Rhine, when you wander afoot from Aachen to Mainz—that is, from Charlemagne to Germany's heyday of glory, under the scepter of the great Barbarossa, your soul must rejoice." In another speech he said: "If one wishes to decide something in the world, it is not the pen alone that will do it if unsupported by the power of the sword." When German troops embarked for China at the time of the Boxer Rebellion (May, 1890) William II advised them: "You are to fight against a cunning, courageous, well-armed, and cruel foe. When you are upon him, know this: Spare nobody, make no prisoners. Use your weapons in a manner to make every Chinaman for a thousand years to come forego the wish to as much as look askance at a German. . . . Give no quarter! Do not rest until the enemy, crushed to the earth, asks pardon on his bended knee. . . . Do honor to the German name, to the flag, and—do not forget it—to me." (*See Reading No. 32.*)

The German people regarded William II as a symbol of national greatness who was to lead them in the vital task of counteracting the diabolical *Einkreisungspolitik* (encirclement policy) of the European Powers. If now and then he struck a discordant note in the Concert of Europe by ill-advised diplomatic action, he was forgiven by his people on the ground that he was Germany's leader in the march to "a place in the sun."

Dismissal of Bismarck, 1890. Disagreement was unavoidable between the elderly chancellor, "who had seen three kings naked," and the impulsive young ruler. The chief cause of difference between the two arose regarding the prolongation of the law against the Socialists. The bill expired in 1890, whereupon Bismarck proposed to make it permanent, but William was opposed to this move on the ground that the disaffection of labor could be removed by remedial measures. In foreign policy, Bismarck hoped to renew the Reinsurance Treaty with Russia, which was due to expire in 1890, but the Emperor would not agree. Moreover, the youthful ruler feared that Bismarck intended to create a "Bismarck dynasty" in the person of his son, Herbert, whom the Chancellor hoped to have as his successor in his important political posts. (*See Reading No. 26.*)

The matter came to a head on a constitutional issue. When Bismarck learned that the Emperor on several occasions had discussed questions of administration with his colleagues without informing him, he drew the attention of the monarch to a Cabinet order of 1852, which had been enacted as a means of giving the Minister-President the complete control that was necessary if he were to be responsible for the whole policy of the government. William replied by commanding Bismarck to draw up a new order reversing the earlier decree. In effect, this proposal would take away from the Chancellor the supreme position that he had enjoyed for so long. Unwilling to countenance this move and regarding it as a degradation of his position, Bismarck declined to obey the command. Bismarck was virtually forced to resign in 1890. The captain of the German ship of state dropped his experienced pilot.

The "New Course." William II's "New Course" called for an intensified colonialism and the construction of a powerful navy as a means of securing Germany's position as a world power. In speech after speech the new Emperor announced that "our future lies on the seas" and "the trident must pass into our hands." There were many reasons for the rise of German navalism. German merchants, economists, and militarists were convinced that a powerful navy constituted the surest protection of foreign commerce and capital investment. The German Navy League was successful in molding public opinion to demand a huge navy. The importance of sea power had been demonstrated to the German people by the American victory in the Spanish-American War and by the British conquest of the Boer republics in South Africa. But above all was the tremendous personal enthusiasm of the Emperor, who was determined to make the German navy the finest in the world. "Our navy," he said, "will grow and flourish, during peaceful times to promote the peaceable interests of the Fatherland, and in war times to destroy the enemy, if God helps us."

The Era of Inept Diplomacy. During his long tenure of office Bismarck had made foreign affairs his exclusive domain and had carefully kept the monarch in the background. William II, careful to maintain his personal rule, appointed a series of weak chancellors: General von Caprivi (1890-1894), an old soldier; Prince Hohenlohe (1894-1900), aged uncle of the emperor; Prince Bernhard von Bülow (1900-1909), a vain courtier whose main efforts were directed to the task of explaining his master's impulsive actions; and Bethmann Hollweg (1909-1917), an inexperienced administrator. For many years the most important director of German policy was the eccentric Fritz von Holstein, councilor at the Foreign Office, who, in the words of S. H. Steinberg, "wove William II's inconsistencies into a supersophisticated pattern, the only recognizable leitmotif of which was that the more waters Germany troubled the more fish she might catch."

Several examples among many betray William II's deplorably inept diplomacy. When in January, 1896, the Jameson Raid collapsed in South Africa, William immediately dispatched a telegram offering his sincere congratulations to President Kruger of the Transvaal Republic. The Kaiser's action was loudly applauded in Germany, but in England it aroused a storm of resentment. Lord Salisbury later (1899) said: "The raid was folly, but the telegram was even more foolish." (*See Reading No. 27.*)

Even more irresponsible was the notorious *Daily Tele-*

graph interview. On October 28, 1908, that newspaper published an account of an interview between William II and an unnamed British subject. Although he sought to present himself as a sincere lover of peace, William, through his own words, showed himself to be an advocate of sheer force in international relations. Seeking to allay British anxiety over Germany's big navy plans, he used arguments that characteristically blended distorted historical fact with offensive flattery. The interview was an unbelievable error that raised a storm of protest in both England and Germany and nearly led to the Kaiser's abdication. (*See Reading No. 28.*)

William II's chaotic foreign policy gradually culminated in the diplomatic isolation of Germany. France, Russia, and England, settling their long-standing differences in the face of the German threat, concluded a series of coalitions culminating in the Triple Entente of 1907. By providing for mutual assistance by the three partners in the event of war with any of the Central Powers, the Triple Entente served as a counteracting force to the Triple Alliance. Europe was now divided into two armed camps, each seeking to maintain the delicate balance of power. Both coalitions began to arm feverishly. (*See Reading No. 25.*)

The Outbreak of World War I. A voluminous literature has been produced in attempts to place responsibility for the outbreak of World War I on particular nations or individuals, but accusations of one kind or another have led to no generally acceptable conclusions. The best possible explanation was given by Lloyd George, who suggested the idea that the nations of Europe, after balancing precariously on the precipice for years, plunged into war without actually wanting it. The basic clues may be found in fundamental causes: the European situation in 1914, charged with an explosive mixture of imperialistic, nationalistic, and militaristic ambitions, burst into flames by spontaneous combustion.

All the major nations contributed to this precarious state of affairs. German industrialists, like those of other nations looking for expansion of foreign markets, supported an intensified imperialism. The theory was that the Germans, a people overflowing with energy and enterprise, deserved an outlet for their accumulated energy. The difficulty was that German imperialism came into headlong conflict with that of other nations. Britain regarded the attempt to promote a Berlin-to-Baghdad railway as an arrow directed at India—the heart of the British Empire. By 1914 the German colonial empire consisted of some 12 million colored people and 24,000 whites in an area of more than a million square miles. While the colonies represented a tremendous investment and there were valuable exports from them, German imperialists insisted that Germany merited a still greater place in the sun.

German efforts to expand in Northwest Africa were met with determined diplomatic resistance. On March 31, 1905, William II visited Tangier, proclaimed Germany's desire for a sovereign and independent Morocco, and demanded equal economic privileges there, a step that resulted in a solid phalanx of opponents. At the Algeciras Conference (January to April, 1906) Britain vigorously supported France. When France in 1911 seized Fez, Germany "for the protection of our interests" dispatched a gunboat to Agadir, but the presence of British and French battleships prevented Germany from occupying Morocco. The Triple Entente was functioning in high gear.

In the involved negotiations immediately preceding the outbreak of war, William II made the grievous error of giving Austria a "blank check" in its relations with Serbia. Events came to a head with the assassination on June 28, 1914, of the Archduke Francis Ferdinand, the heir presumptive to the throne of Austria-Hungary, in Sarajevo, the capital of Bosnia. Germany declared war on Russia on August 1 and on France on August 3.

Germany in World War I. Seldom has a nation gone to war in a greater outburst of enthusiasm and with greater confidence than did the Germans in 1914. William II's slogan: "No more parties, Germans all!" was recognized even by the Socialists, who enthusiastically joined the national front. The Reichstag unanimously voted war credits. German scholars almost to a man announced that they would not abandon the Fatherland in its hour of need and heatedly denied that there was anything wrong in violating Belgian neutrality. (*See Reading No. 35.*) The British were denounced in a concentrated campaign of national hate, culminating in Ernst Lissauer's *Hymn of Hate* (*see Reading No. 34*):

> Hate by water and hate by land,
> Hate by heart and hate of the hand,
> We love as one, we hate as one,
> We have one foe, and one alone—ENGLAND!

The German public exuberantly celebrated the early victories of the perfectly trained German armies, not realizing that these triumphs were bought at the price of failures in strategy.

According to the prearranged Schlieffen Plan, the German armies in early August, 1914, invaded Belgium with the object of swinging like a hammer in a wide arc on Paris. The violation of the neutrality of Belgium, which had been guaranteed by the European powers in 1839, brought England into the war immediately. (*See Readings Nos. 11 and 33.*) At the critical First Battle of the Marne (September 6-14, 1914) the Schlieffen plan was smashed when Helmuth von Moltke became alarmed, detached several divisions from his right wing to be sent to the east, and thereby weakened the striking power of his seven colossal armies. The war was actually lost within these first few weeks. The Germans were deprived of the chance for a stalemate at the Battle of Jutland (May 31-June 16, 1916). Although the German fleet claimed victory, it retired to Kiel and remained there for the duration of the war. The introduction of the convoy system by the British in 1917 was successful in counteracting Germany's U-boat campaign and placed at the disposal of the Allied Powers the overpowering resources of the United States.

At the outbreak of war the vast Russian armies poured into East Prussia and Galicia and turned like a giant steam-roller on Berlin. Led by Generals Rennenkampf and Samsonov, two separate armies, operating without liaison, went down to one of the most dramatic defeats in history. The Germans, under Generals Ludendorff and Hindenburg, drove a wedge between the two armies, annihilated one at Tannenberg (August 26-30, 1914), and bottled up the other at the Masurian Lakes (September 5-15, 1914). The Russians lost a quarter of a million men and an enormous quantity of supplies.

Despite stalemate in the West and victory in the East, Germany had lost the initiative for a quick and decisive victory over the Allies. As German morale began to sag, William II dismissed General Falkenhayn and called the team of Hindenburg and Ludendorff to the command of the German armies in August, 1916. Not only did these generals assume military command, but they also took over actual control of important political decisions. The Emperor gradually receded into the background. The remainder of the war took place under what amounted to a Ludendorff dictatorship; the stubborn, arrogant, and ruthless general controlled nearly all phases of military and civilian rule.

Germany was in no position to wage a long-drawn-out war. Dependent upon imports for food and strategic materials, she was seriously hurt by the British blockade, and by the necessity of fighting a two-front war. German manpower dwindled alarmingly. That Germany was able to hold out for four years may be attributed to the remarkable discipline of the people, the organizational capacity of the leaders, and the ingenuity of German scientists. Once it became clear that Germany this time would not win her traditionally quick and overwhelming triumph, the people were beset by war weariness and the home front began to collapse.

Several proposals for peace had been made as early as 1916. In the opening months of 1917 the German Social Democratic leaders, aware of popular discontent, declared that it was willing to support a just peace. On August 1, 1917, Pope Benedict XV, grieved by the horrors of the terrible conflict, urged a just and honorable peace, but the German government, hoping for a miracle, ignored his entreaties. On January 8, 1918, President Wilson issued a statement of Allied war aims, the Fourteen Points, which had a tremendous effect on war-weary Germany and gave the Germans the impression that they could have a peace of reconstruction rather than one of revenge.

In the meantime a combination of military reverses, incompetent leadership, and popular disaffection had led in March, 1917, to a revolution in Russia and her eventual retirement from the war. (*See Reading No. 37.*) On April 6, 1917, the United States entered the war and

with its vast manpower and resources, thrown with un-
expected speed into the conflict, tipped the scales in
favor of the Allies. (*See Reading No. 36.*) The Ludendorff offensive starting in March, 1918, was decisively
smashed at the Second Battle of the Marne (July 15-
August 7, 1918). Beaten on the battlefield, their supplies
diminishing to a vanishing point, and the home front in
a state of disintegration, the Germans signed an armistice
in a railway car at Compiègne on November 11, 1918.

On June 28, 1919, a German delegation reluctantly
signed the Treaty of Versailles at the Hall of Mirrors
in the palace at Versailles, where in 1871 the German
Empire had been proclaimed by Bismarck. The territorial
terms included: the transfer of all German colonies to
the Allies as mandates; the cession of Alsace-Lorraine to
France; award of the Polish Corridor to Poland and
Memel to the Allies; provisions for plebiscites in North
Schleswig and Upper Silesia; and cession, after a plebi-
scite, of Eupen, Malmédy, and Moresnet to Belgium.
The military and naval clauses included: Allied occupation of the Rhineland, with provisions for gradual retirement; limitation of the German army to 100,000 men;
abolition of conscription; limitation of the German
navy to six battleships, six light cruisers, twelve destroyers, and twelve torpedo boats; elimination of the
German air force; restriction of German munitions;
prohibition of poison gas; and demolition of German
fortifications along the North and Baltic Seas. According
to the economic clauses, Germany, on the basis of Article
231, the war-guilt clause, was held responsible along
with her allies for all the damages of the war. Furthermore, payment of the expenses of the army of occupation
was to be made by Germany; German foreign investments
and property in Allied countries were confiscated; Allied
citizens were guaranteed equal commercial rights in
Germany; the Elbe, Oder, Niemen, and Danube rivers
were placed under international control; Germany was
to pay for all animals, securities, and other objects confiscated during the war; and works of art and trophies
were to be returned. In Germany all political parties
united to denounce the settlement as the *Diktat* of Versailles, as a Carthaginian peace designed to destroy Germany and remove her from the family of nations. In the

Allied countries, on the other hand, it was believed that
Germany had received fair and just treatment for an
unsuccessful attempt to smash her way to world power.
(*See Reading No. 38.*)

— 11 —

FROM THE WEIMAR REPUBLIC
THROUGH NAZI
TOTALITARIANISM, 1919-1957

The German Revolution. With Germany on the
verge of defeat, William II, on October 3, 1918, appointed
his cousin, Prince Max of Baden as Chancellor. President
Wilson, however, refused to deal with any other than a
popular government. When the armistice was signed on
November 7, Germany was already in the throes of
revolution, beginning at Kiel where the sailors refused
to sail on a last, desperate suicide mission. In a few days
revolution overran the whole of Germany. Anxious to
avert the proclamation of a Soviet republic, Scheidemann,
the Social Democratic deputy, proclaimed the German
Republic on November 9. The Emperor abdicated and
fled to Holland. A federation of republican states, temporarily headed by a council of six People's Commissars
(three Majority Socialists and three Independent Socialists) was created under the joint chairmanship of
Ebert and Haase. When the Independent Socialists bolted,
the Majority Socialists took over. The Spartacists, the
Communist party, sought to extend the revolution into a
dictatorship of the proletariat, but the Social Democrats
left the task of crushing them to Gustav Noske, "the
bloodhound of the Revolution." Karl Liebknecht and
Rosa Luxemburg, Spartacist leaders, were killed.

Thus, within the space of a few weeks, Germany was

transformed from a semi-autocratic monarchy, first into a parliamentary monarchy and then into a semi-socialist republic. The "Revolution" of 1918 was in no sense a mass movement against the monarchy, but rather a kind of ineffective improvisation in a vacuum. Both German people and leaders were indecisive at this critical moment. This made-to-order revolution was conceived in despair and humiliation, imposed upon Germany from the outside, unwanted and unloved.

The Weimar Republic. Similarly, the Weimar Republic was burdened from its very beginning with the odium and odor of defeat. Not only were the German people ill-prepared for any advanced form of democracy but the victor powers, which at one time had made a careful distinction between the German people and their reactionary rulers, now showed little sympathy or understanding for the fledgling republic. The Weimar Republic suffered humiliation after humiliation at the hands of the victor powers. Germans fiercely resented the Republic as an illegitimate child of defeat and came to regard it as synonymous with national disgrace. In the words of A. J. P. Taylor, the first four years of the Weimar Republic "were consumed in the political and economic confusion which followed the Four Years' War; in its last three years there was a temporary dictatorship half clothed in legality, which reduced the republic to a sham long before it was openly overthrown." The Germans did not seem to be able to grasp the differences between the sufferings contingent to defeat and the sufferings related directly to war. They resented the continued occupation of German territory, the retention of German war prisoners, and the maintenance of the naval blockade, all of which they associated with the new Republic and the *Gewaltfrieden*.

The political system set up by the Weimar Constitution was based in parts on the American, British, French, and Swiss forms of government. On paper the new constitution was one of the most advanced in the history of mankind, but its effectiveness was almost destroyed by Article 48, which permitted the President to lift the entire bill of rights in emergencies. In thus permitting the suspension of fundamental rights, the Constitution could be invalidated in spirit at the whim of the executive. The Constitution provided for a President elected by direct vote of the people for a term of seven years, after which he was eligible for reelection. Actual executive authority was vested in a ministry headed by the Chancellor, appointed by the President, but responsible to the Reichstag. The Reichstag, elected for a period of four years, could initiate legislation. The old Reichsrat, representing the states, was retained, but in a position of secondary importance. A comprehensive bill of rights insured the legal equality of all sexes, established free and compulsory education up to the age of eighteen, and provided for a system of social legislation. (*See Reading No. 39.*)

From its beginning the Weimar Republic was burdened by political disaffection from both right and left. Irreconcilable nationalists, monarchists, and militarists organized terroristic societies for the purpose of overthrowing the Republic. On March 13, 1920, a group of reactionaries supported by Ludendorff and led by Kapp, an obscure Prussian official, marched on Berlin and compelled President Ebert to flee, but the putsch failed when the workers of Berlin paralyzed the capital by a general strike. In the Reichstag elections of June, 1920, republican political power shrank still further. Fanatical members of reactionary societies murdered many of the political leaders, including Matthias Erzberger, Centrist statesman who had signed the Treaty of Versailles, and Walter Rathenau, the brilliant Jewish organizer of the national economy in the war, who was regarded as a traitor because he supported the cause of international conciliation.

The political chaos reflected a grave economic situation. German industry was badly dislocated—during the war the national debt had grown thirtyfold and the burden of reparations imposed at Versailles helped to deteriorate what was already a collapsing economy. In January, 1923, when Germany failed to meet her reparations payments as prescribed in the Treaty of Versailles, the French occupied the Ruhr Valley. The effect on the German mark was almost immediate. The mark fell to a third of a thousand-billionth part of its 1913 value; some 1500 printing companies ran their presses twenty-four hours a day to print enough paper money to keep up with the inflation. The German economy was shattered from top to bottom. The middle class, backbone of the German economy, was virtually destroyed, and it became ripe for the blandishments of chauvinists. The Dawes Plan of 1924 stabilized the mark through issuance of the Rentenmark, but untold damage was already done.

In the midst of the Ruhr occupation, General Ludendorff and an obscure Austrian house painter, Adolf Hitler, staged a comic-opera putsch at a beerhall in Munich, capital of Bavaria. The Hitler-Ludendorff revolt, although quickly suppressed by the Reichswehr, nevertheless betrayed the basic weakness of the Republic. In August, 1923, Gustav Stresemann became Chancellor and for six years directed German diplomacy in ten different cabinets. Stresemann called for fulfillment of the Versailles Treaty, signed the Locarno treaties in 1925 accepting the territorial provisions of Versailles, and in 1926 led Germany into the League of Nations. Admirers praised Stresemann as a diplomat genuinely desirous of having Germany fulfill her international obligations, while critics denounced him as "an artful deceiver" who worked to prepare his country for a war of revenge. The Stresemann era witnessed a striking economic recovery. As confidence in Germany's future returned, Western capitalists poured loans into the German economy. In rebuilding German industry, American techniques of large-scale manufacturing were successfully used. The government maintained the traditional policy of paternalism not only in industry, but in housing, agriculture, and labor relations. Economic recovery progressed by leaps and bounds, until the world-wide depression of 1929 hit Germany with devastating force. The German economy, built to a large extent on foreign loans, was hit hard by the stoppage of foreign funds. Added to this was the fear of another inflation, which led many Germans to hoard their money or transfer it abroad. Once again the masses were plunged into despair.

In 1925, on the death of President Ebert, Field Marshal Paul von Hindenburg, the hero of Tannenberg, was elected to the presidency. In foreign capitals this was regarded as the first step in the restoration of the Hohenzollerns and a possible war of revenge, but the old soldier took seriously his oath to uphold the constitution and supported the Weimar democracy until 1932. In the Reichstag elections of 1930, the National Socialist vote increased from 800,000 to nearly 6.5 millions, from 12 to 107 deputies, an indication that the German people desperately desired new leadership. The country was in a grave financial crisis with millions of Germans on relief. An American reporter estimated at this time that a quarter of the population did not have enough to eat, and that a family of three living on state aid had the equivalent of little more than four dollars a month for food, after paying for rent, heat, and light.

Foreign Policy. German foreign policy after World War I revolved around relations with Russia. By the accident of geography Germany had been caught between East and West, the central fact of her historical experience. The linchpin of the whole European system, she played East and West off against one another in an attempt to avoid the consequences of Versailles. Rapprochement between Germany and Russia began in the 1920's and lasted until 1934. There was an important *quid pro quo:* Russia needed German political and technical help for her internal reconstruction as well as a *point d'appui,* a foothold in the enemy's camp. The two outcasts of Europe joined forces in the Russo-German Treaty of Rapallo, signed early in 1922. Thereafter Germany, having obtained certain concessions from the West, turned away from Russia (Locarno Pact, 1925) and then swung back again. The relationship varied: in 1925-26 the swing was very slight; in 1929-30 it was perceptibly greater; in 1931-39 it was plain for all to see. In late 1931, Rapallo gradually was overshadowed by the growth of Nazism and the emergence of a German right wing under Brüning that had no use for Soviet Russia. When in 1934 Hitler categorically rejected Russian overtures for a continuation of the old relationship, Stalin threw in his lot with the Western powers. This was the end of Rapallo, but not the end of Russia's capitalist *point d'appui,* which was revived by the Hitler-Stalin Pact of 1939. After 1945 Germany once more became a pawn between East and West.

The Emergence of National Socialism. The economic catastrophe of 1930 does not by itself explain the rise of National Socialism, though it is true that unemployment and misery contributed heavily. The impoverished middle and lower classes, seeking some haven in the economic storm, turned to a fanatical demagogue because he promised a quick end to their discontent. There was widespread contempt for the Weimar Republic because of its inability to cure economic ills and because it seemed to make little headway in returning Germany to the status of a Great Power. Monarchists and professional soldiers saw in Nazism a means of serving their own special aims. The farmers were impressed by Nazi pledges to dissolve the large Junker estates, the workers were attracted by Hitler's promise to shatter the bonds of *Zinsknechtschaft* (interest-servitude). Property-holding Germans saw in National Socialism the best answer to an encroaching communism. Thousands of doctors of philosophy without jobs saw in Hitler the magician who would lead them to a better way of life. The youth of Germany was hypnotized by the circus-like atmosphere of Nazism; women were intrigued by what they believed to be the physical beauty of *der schoene Adolf;* anti-Semites were attracted by Hitler's passionate denunciation of the Jews and by his racial mythology. Hitler had a ready answer for all German ills: he was the Siegfried who would avenge the defeat of 1918 and lead the discontented Germans to prosperity. (*See Reading No. 40.*)

Adolf Hitler was born at Branau, Austria, on April 20, 1889. The character is a familiar one in every German *Bierstube.* Self-educated, shrewd, arrogant, he held forth on every subject under the sun, from food to world politics, from music to military tactics. Pompous and omniscient, he refused to discuss any ideas, but instead issued dicta and ukases. He mistook his intuitions for scientific fact. He claimed to know all the answers to the meaning of history. He lived in a curious dream world, dismissing as insane anyone who disagreed with his judgments and disconnected monologues. Through roundabout means he absorbed the irrational ideas of Gobineau's *Essay on the Inequality of Human Races,* Houston Stewart Chamberlain's *Foundations of the Nineteenth Century,* Alfred Rosenberg's *Myth of the Twentieth Century,* and ill-digested interpretations of Nietzsche, Schopenhauer, Spengler, Haushofer, Frederick the Great, and Carlyle. H. R. Trever-Roper, the British historian, describes this sick mind: "A terrible phenomenon, imposing indeed in its granite harshness and yet infinitely squalid in its miscellaneous cumber—like some huge barbarian monolith, the expression of giant strength and savage genius, surrounded by a festering heap of refuse—old tins and dead vermin, ashes and eggshells and ordure—the intellectual *detritus* of centuries." It is becoming increasingly clear that an understanding of the mind of Hitler cannot be achieved by the historian without the assistance of the psychologist, the psychiatrist, and the psychoanalyst. (*See Readings No. 41-45.*)

Nazi Totalitarianism. Once in power, Hitler moved astutely and ruthlessly to consolidate his authoritarian state. Assuming absolute political authority, he required members of the German armed forces to take a personal oath of allegiance to him. He retained the form of the Reichstag, which became merely a body to echo his will. Although the electorate was given the privilege of infrequent plebiscites, it had no voice in the Third Reich. Hitler dissolved the trade unions and confiscated their property and funds; he made the administration of justice, once the pride of Germany, subservient to Nazi aims. He coordinated every phase of national life, including church, press, education, industry, and army, in the Nazi Reich, which, he boasted, would last for a thousand years. He abrogated all individual rights guaranteed by the Weimer constitution. A shocked world witnessed his barbaric campaign "to protect German honor" against the Jews, who, numbering only about one per cent of the population, were accused of responsibility for all German ills. Opponents of the regime were thrust into concentration camps, where they were subjected to bestial horrors. On June 30, 1934, Hitler, in a barbaric blood-purge, liquidated several hundred of his followers who had wanted to extend the revolution into a second—socialist—phase.

Hitler placed all economic matters under state control. He solved the problem of unemployment by dismissing enemies of the state, decreeing compulsory military service, providing for extensive public works, and organizing slave labor camps. He obtained funds for the remilitarization of Germany by a system of forced loans from banks, industries, and insurance companies and by suspending payment on foreign debts. He forced neighboring small countries to accept barter agreements which worked to the advantage of the German economic system.

The German people were placed in the strait jacket of cultural uniformity. All cultural activities were thoroughly coordinated and subordinated to Nazi ideology. "The whole function of education," said the Nazi Minister for Culture and Education, "is to create a Nazi." All German culture was to imbue German citizens with the ideas of glorification of the Leader, fanatical worship of the Fatherland, intolerant racial prejudice, blind obedience, hatred for Jews, and zest for war. Germany rapidly sank in the quicksand of intellectual provincialism. Scientific manpower was drained from the universities by emigration of scholars. Germany's reputation as a cultural leader of Europe suffered a precipitous decline.

When the Nazis sought to coordinate religious organizations in the totalitarian state, they met strong resistance. Hitler arrested pastors and priests alike and threw them into concentration camps; he organized a new form of "positive Christianity" as a means of splitting Protestantism; he violated a concordat made in 1933 with the Catholic Church by which he had promised that Catholics would not be molested as long as they did not take part in politics. In the meantime Nazis sought a substitute for the traditional religions by organizing neo-pagan cults based on "blood-race-soil," preaching racial superiority, and practicing the rites of ancient Teutonic mythology.

Estimate of Nazism.   In describing the Nazi regime a conscientious historian, Koppel S. Pinson, titled his chapter: "Germany Goes Berserk, 1933-1945." It is a fair historical judgment. Pinson found it "almost impossible to describe the diabolical perversity, the wild flights of political fantasy, the enormity of the crimes committed and the disaster and ruin brought both to Germany and the entire world." [1] The Nazi era, in coldly objective terms, represented a descent into bestiality and vulgarization such as the world had never witnessed before in all its history. Nazism has been described as "a crude, irreducible atavism," as "surrealism in politics and demagogy." In the words of Stephen Roberts, it was "a reversion to the oldest state of affairs of which our

[1] Koppel S. Pinson, *Modern Germany* (New York, 1954) p. 479.

anthropologists have any knowledge. . . . It reconstructed
the taboo system, the system in which every part of the
social structure depends on the unquestioning acceptance
of the edicts of the priests. . . . The Nazis resurrected
tribal instincts in the mystical sanctions of a savage
society." [2]

How was it possible for such a highly civilized people
as the Germans to allow themselves to be caught in this
totalitarian strait jacket? According to one of Germany's
greatest historians, Friedrich Meinecke, it was a "sudden
catastrophe" which had "certain analogies and precedents
in the authoritarian systems of neighboring countries."
Seldom has a distinguished scholar been more wrong in
his analysis of an historical movement. Nazi extremism
was not a bolt out of the heavens, nor did it occur in a
vacuum. Behind it was a long tradition; its roots lay deep
in history. It was the result of a national tradition of
discipline and obedience, ground into the Germans by
a combination of Hegelian worship of the State, Prussian
intransigence, militarism, nationalism, romanticism, and
historicism. The Germans who were shocked and amazed
by the excesses of Hitlerism never understood that the
political regime that had led them almost to destruction
was the logical outcome of a long and dangerous intellectual tradition. Despite its claims of historical novelty
in seeking to combine the waves of nationalism and
socialism, the Nazi movement in reality was stale and
unoriginal—it was simple tyranny. There was little new
in Nazism other than the fanatical and ferocious methods
used to implement its ideology.

Originally a bit skeptical about this comic-opera
charlatan, the German people began to see in him a leader
who would guide them out of the misery of the past to
a glorious future. More and more they began to be convinced of Hitler's infallibility as he delivered one crippling
blow after another to the system of Versailles. Politically
illiterate Germans had no understanding of what was
happening to them. It was necessary to invent a new
name—genocide—for a stupendous crime against humanity—the slaughtering of millions of Jews by asphyxiation
in gas ovens. The massacre of other millions, the devital-

[2] S. H. Roberts, *The House that Hitler Built* (New York,
1939) Part I, Chap. IV.

ization of nations, the inhuman atrocities, all these horrors led the world to believe that the German nation had taken leave of its senses. It took a world-wide coalition to convince the Germans that "Nazi dynamism" was a snare and a delusion and to smash their second bid for world domination.

Germany in World War II. Historians today generally distribute responsibility for the outbreak of World War I to several nations, but most of them agree that the blame for *starting* World War II rests solely and squarely on Germany. (*See Reading No. 46.*) The basic causes of World Wars I and II were similar, but the immediate cause of World War II was the continued aggressions of Nazi Germany. Hitler was obsessed with the idea that the superior German race was destined to rule mankind; he was ready to smash his way to world domination or perish in the attempt. "For the good of the German people," he said, "we must wish for a war every fifteen or twenty years." At the same time, he informed the world: "I am not crazy enough to want a war." At a secret meeting held on November 5, 1937, Hitler outlined to his military leaders the practical steps in undertaking aggression against other countries. Colonel Hossbach, who took minutes at the meeting, reported: "If the *Fuehrer* is still living, then it will be his irrevocable decision to solve the German space-problem no later than 1943-45. . . . The question for Germany is where the greatest possible conquest can be made at lowest cost." Geoffrey Bruun states that "with a man as erratic and as intoxicated with power as the German chancellor no just and reasonable peace was possible, no engagement durable, no pledge secure. As Hitler's arrogance increased he discarded the pretense of mutual bargaining and summoned statesmen to his presence to hear his decisions."

Hitler's foreign policy was an extraordinary exercise in international blackmail. In March, 1935, he announced the rearmament of Germany, reintroduced conscription, and enlarged the army, navy, and air force. In 1936 German troops marched into the Rhineland. In 1938, in order "to preserve Austria," he formally incorporated that state into the Third Reich. On September 29, 1938, Czechoslovakia was sold down the river and partially dismembered, a betrayal that meant the end of collective security. On September 1, 1939, Hitler sent his armies crashing into Poland, making a scrap of paper of Chamberlain's assurance from Hitler that German territorial ambitions were now satisfied after Munich. Several days earlier, on August 22, 1939, Chamberlain wrote to Hitler: "It has been alleged that, if His Majesty's Government had made their position more clear in 1914, the great catastrophe would have been avoided. His Majesty's Government are resolved that on this occasion there shall be no such tragic misunderstanding." Hitler was so certain of his destiny that he paid no attention to this clear-cut warning. "In starting and making a war," he said, "it is not right that matters, but victory."

The Nazi *Fuehrer* had counted on a short war. For over three years he went from one victory to another. The period of the "phony war" in the West was shattered in April, 1940, when Hitler invaded Denmark, Norway, Belgium, Holland, and Luxemburg. In June, 1940, France, weakened by internal dissension, defeatism, and treason, succumbed to the Nazis. The masses of the German people, who had gone to war without that exuberance shown in 1914, nevertheless were delighted by Hitler's triumphs, which made him the greatest conqueror of modern times. A new European order under the German "master race" seemed to be in the process of formation. (*See Reading No. 47.*)

But this wild dream was shattered on the rocks of British and Russian resistance. Hitler lost the savage air battle of Britain, when the English, standing virtually alone, smashed Göring's *Luftwaffe* in the skies. On June 22, 1941, Hitler, who had boasted in *Mein Kampf* that he would never make the error of fighting on two fronts at the same time, astonished the world by invading Russia in a *Blitzkrieg*. At first victorious, he soon found his armies trapped in Russia very much as Napoleon had been caught. The Japanese attack on Pearl Harbor on December 7, 1941, brought the United States into the war, thereby sealing the doom of the Nazi state.

The record of Nazi brutalities in the conquered states of Europe and the parallel atrocities visited upon the Jews form one of the most depressing pages of history.

Entire communities were wiped out, hostages were executed, and able-bodied men were herded into slave-labor camps to keep the wheels of the German armaments industry rolling. "I have sent to the East," Hitler said, "only my 'Death Head Units' with the order to kill without mercy all men, women and children of Polish race or language. Only in such a way will we win the vital space that we need. Who still talks nowadays of the extermination of the Armenians?" This policy backfired. Russians, suffering under the Stalin slave state, at first turned to Hitler as a liberator, but when the Nazi *Fuehrer* adopted his usual policy of brutal terrorization the Russians rallied to the patriotic defense of their fatherland.

The defeat at Stalingrad in February, 1943, Allied mastery of the air, the invasion of Normandy by a huge Allied force on June 6, 1944, and the Battle for Germany in early 1945 culminated in the defeat of Nazi Germany. Germany lost 3,250,000 battle dead and spent $272,900,-000,000 in the most costly conflict in history. The suicide of Hitler, Himmler, and Goebbels, and the result of the Nuremberg trials which condemned other Nazi war criminals to death, provided small atonement for the crimes committed by the Nazi state. (*See Readings No. 48 and 49.*)

Germany Since 1945. For the second time in a century Germany's dream of expansion was shattered. This time the costs were terrifying in their enormity: millions killed and wounded, a host of men missing in action or captured, and German cities in ruins. It was as if an entire country had been laid waste by a gigantic scythe. Göring had boasted that not one single Allied bomber would get through to Berlin, but at the end of the war a reporter noted that "Berlin can now be regarded only as a geographical location heaped with mountainous mounds of debris." The entire country was in chaos, the system of transportation broken down, the government not functioning, the population disorganized. It was almost as if a scene from Dante's *Inferno* had come to life.

The German people, stunned and bewildered, seemed mentally unable to comprehend the extent of the catastrophe. There was no revolution: Germany once more was freed by outsiders. There had been little psychological preparation for the calamity. Accustomed to taking orders from above and acting in a disciplined manner, the Germans were now apathetical in the absence of firm leadership. Traditional German morality had collapsed under the shock of defeat.

At Potsdam the Allies divided Germany into four zones of control—American, British, Russian, and French, cutting across the old state and provincial boundaries. (*See Reading No. 50.*) Greater Berlin was split into four similar sectors, forming a fifth zone and a bone of contention between Soviet Russia and the West. The occupying authorities began the task of denazifying, demilitarizing, decartelizing, and democratizing Germany, a goal considerably weakened by increasing friction between the Soviet Union and the West.

In the West the Federal Republic of Germany, embracing slightly more than half the area of prewar Germany but nearly three-quarters of its population, was created with its capital at Bonn. In September, 1949, Dr. Theodor Heuss was elected first president of the Bonn Republic. A federal parliament, based on that of the Weimar Republic, was set up. On May 26, 1952, West Germany was integrated into the North Atlantic Alliance and entered the community of free nations as an equal partner. Leadership in West Germany was entrusted to the hands of elderly Chancellor Konrad Adenauer.

Economic Recovery. In 1945 Germany was a defeated, broken country. A decade later the West German economy attained a recovery almost without parallel in history. Unemployment was reduced; the currency reserve rose tremendously; public finances, showing surpluses despite tax reductions, became the envy of Europe; production rose rapidly.

The statistics of German recovery speak for themselves. By 1953 West Germany achieved an industrial output 59% higher than in 1936. Her gold and dollar reserves in late 1956 totalled $3.7 billion, as against Britain's $2.2 billion. By 1952 she was the largest creditor in the European Payment Plan with an accumulated credit of almost $480 millions. The story in exports, key to industrial health, is striking. From 1951 to 1956 West German exports tripled in value, closing in on second-place

Britain and first-place United States. In 1955 West Germany had a trade *surplus* of $286 million, while Britain had a deficit of $985 million. West Germany's share of manufactured exports rose from 13.3 to 15.6 per cent from 1954 to 1956, at a time when Britain's dropped from 21.3 to 19.8 per cent. German car exports increased from $54 million in 1950 to $331 million in 1955, while Britain's only rose from $301 million to $316 million. The German *Volkswagen* began to conquer the small-car markets of the world; complete assembly plants for the German automobile were set up all over the world. West Germany now sells more bicycles in the United States than Britain, which once had a virtual monopoly on foreign bicycle sales. West Germany went ahead of Britain for the No. 1 trading position in South America. Her chemical exports passed that of Britain for the first time.

To some extent this remarkable phenomenon was due to American aid of some $3.4 billion dollars, as well as hard work, but other countries also worked zealously and received American aid with far less spectacular results. The recovery of West Germany is a classic case of the free-market economy operating successfully with a limited number of strategically selected controls, and greatly helped by political and economic events outside Germany's borders. Economic life was carefully planned and managed by the government. The new German leaders apparently did the right things and had the good luck to do them at the right time.

Some observers attribute the beaver-like activity of contemporary Germans to a desperate search to forget the past and to sublimate their guilt feelings by a highly neurotic concern for work, work, and more work. Since 1945 the Germans have paid but little attention to other than economic pursuits: politics and culture have received only marginal attention. Whatever the reason, the Germans rapidly rose to the top of the European economic structure, with German goods once again flowing to the markets of the world and the mark widely recognized as one of the most stable European hard currencies. To many it seemed to be an economic miracle.

The East German Republic presented a striking contrast to the economic recovery of the Bonn Republic.

Containing 27% of Germany's population and 31% of its area, East Germany became in effect a satellite state of the Soviet Union. Economic conditions sank to the level of the Soviet Union. Non-Communist parties were permitted to have a nominal existence, but a People's Police, nucleus of an army, carefully watched all dissenters. Refugees by the thousands crossed the "green border" to the West. In June, 1953, there was a serious uprising against Communist rule in East Berlin, the first revolt of the century by the workers themselves against a government claiming to be based on the working masses.

The German Question. The support of West Germany by the United States and other Western Powers was a calculated risk. Some observers condemn the whole German past and the German people and hold that it is impossible to bring this nation for any length of time into the civilized community. Others believe that Germany is now only "a burnt-out crater of great *Machtpolitik*" and that she should be accepted as an ally in a possible struggle for power with the Soviet Union.

Inside Germany itself German intellectuals racked their brains to find an answer for their country's descent into barbarism. A few examined their consciences and admitted responsibility. Rudolf Pechel wrote: "It is and remains a fact that Hitler and his regime unloosed the war, hurled the entire world into unspeakable misery, annihilated millions of lives, attempted to exterminate the Jews with the most gruesome means, and placed all who did not conform to his views under the axe and on the rack of the executioner. The fact remains that the German people are co-responsible for this crime." Others, notably former politicians and political figures such as Ernst von Weiszäcker, Herbert von Dirksen, and Erich Kordt, published memoirs attributing Hitlerism to "unpardonable errors" and "unfortunate provocations" of other countries. On the other hand, some German historians have begun to understand the meaning and consequences of historicism, State-worship, and blood-and-iron implicit in the rigid conservatism of Bismarck and the irrationalism of Hitler. Joachim Leuschner describes Hitlerism as "the last step from nationality to bestiality," and adds: "Moreover, the gas chambers of Auschwitz belong to our national heritage; without recognition, atonement, and the surmounting of this national disgrace there can be no new dignity for our people."

There are, indeed, some hopeful signs that Germans are seeking ways to integrate themselves into the West and thus provide a new opportunity for their creative contribution to a common civilization based on a common heritage. At the same time, there persist in Germany the relics of an authoritarian past; open admiration for Nazi leaders has begun to reappear, and books like Ernst von Salomon's *Fragebogen,* a paean to the old nationalism, have enjoyed widespread success. The dilemma—a free, united, and democratic Germany, or a nationalistic, authoritarian Germany, the open or closed society—is not yet resolved.

This dilemma, part and parcel of what has been called "the German Question," has been of critical importance not only for the German people but for the entire world. Germany has remained an obstreperous, unhappy stepchild among nations. Responsible for this phenomenon is a combination of peculiar historical and psychological factors. Throughout her tragic history, Germany, situated in the heartland of Europe but with no natural or defensible barriers to hold her firmly together, has been desperately and vainly seeking the road to cohesion. She has vacillated between being despised as a helpless buffer state and being feared and hated as a violent and predatory power.

Psychologically, the German people remained suspended in uneasy limbo between East and West. German culture accepted some ideas and idealism from the West, while rejecting others. The result was a sense of national frustration, guilt-ridden, anxious, hostile. Politically immature and beset by a sense of insecurity, the Germans overcompensated by turning to any father-image who seemed to satisfy their needs—from *"der alte Fritz"* to William of the iron fist to the hypomanic Hitler. The vacillations were always erratic—a people who provided a model of neatness and cleanliness was weak and foolish enough to fall into the hands of Nazi madmen. The Germany which produced Goethe, Lessing, and Bach also produced Banse, Himmler, and Streicher. The executioners at the crematoria of Belsen performed their macabre duties to the music of Beethoven. Germans saw nothing wrong in self-pity when the ruin visited on other cities from the air was visited on themselves.

The German Question remains unsolved. It is to be hoped, however, that a unified Germany, free and secure, may finally take its place in a peaceful world.

Part II

READINGS

— Reading No. 1 —

TACITUS ON THE EARLY GERMANS, 98 A.D. *

In his Germania, *C. Cornelius Tacitus, the Roman historian, gave a valuable description of the early Germans. It is probable that he exaggerated the virtues of the Germans in order to stress what he felt to be the degeneration of his fellow Romans. As Rousseau later proclaimed the virtues of the "noble savage," so Tacitus praised the morality, individualism, and courage of the blond giants from the north.*

꜒   ꜒   ꜒

For my own part, I agree with those who think that the tribes of Germany are free from all trace of intermarriage with foreign nations, and that they appear as a distinct, unmixed race, like none but themselves. Hence it is that the same physical features are to be observed throughout so vast a population. All have fierce blue eyes, reddish hair, and huge bodies fit only for sudden exercise. They are not very able to endure labor that is exhausting. Heat and thirst they cannot withstand at all, though to cold and hunger their soil and climate have hardened them.

In battle it is considered shameful for the chief to allow any of his followers to excel him in valor, and for the followers not to equal their chief in deeds of bravery. To survive the chief and return from the field is a disgrace and a reproach for life. To defend and protect him, and to add to his renown by courageous fighting is the height of loyalty. The chief fights for victory; his companions

* C. Cornelius Tacitus, *De origine, situ, moribus ac populis Germanorum* [*The Germania*], Chaps. 2-24, *passim.* Adapted from the translation by Alfred J. Church and William J. Broadribb (London, 1868) pp. 1-16.

must fight for the chief. If their native state sinks into the sloth of peace and quiet many noble youths voluntarily seek those tribes which are waging some war, both because inaction is disliked by their race and because it is in war that they win renown most readily. . . . They actually think it tame and stupid to acquire by sweat or toil what they may win by their blood.

When not engaged in war they pass much of their time in the chase, and still more in idleness, giving themselves up to sleep and feasting. The bravest and most warlike do no work; they give over the management of the household, of the home, and of the land to the women, the old men, and the weaker members of the family, while they themselves remain in the most sluggish inactivity. . . .

At all their gatherings there is one and the same kind of amusement. This is the dancing of naked youths amid swords and lances that all the time endanger their lives. Experience gives them skill, and skill in turn gives them grace. They scorn to receive profit or pay, for, however reckless their pastime, its reward is only the pleasure of the spectators. Strangely enough, they make games of chance a serious employment, even when sober, and so venturesome are they about winning or losing that, when every other resource has failed, on the final throw of the dice they will stake even their freedom. He who loses goes into voluntary slavery. . . .

— Reading No. 2 —

EINHARD ON CHARLEMAGNE, c. 800*

Charlemagne (768-814), whose name is an old French form for the Latin Carolus Magnus (Charles the Great), was the first Germanic figure of whom we possess any satisfactory historical knowledge. Einhard (or Eginhard), companion and secretary to the Frankish ruler, wrote the following description of Charlemagne.

In accordance with the national custom, he took frequent exercise on horseback and in the chase, in which sports scarcely any people in the world can equal the Franks. . . . He was temperate in eating, and especially so in drinking. . . . While at the table, he listened to reading or music, the subjects of the readings being the stories and deeds of olden time. . . . He had the gift of ready and fluent speech, and could express whatever he had to say with the utmost clearness . . . so . . . eloquent indeed was he that he might have been taken for a teacher of oratory. He most zealously cherished the liberal arts, held those that taught them in great esteem, and conferred great honors on them. . . . He spent much time and labor studying rhetoric, dialectic, and especially astronomy. . . . He also tried to write, and used to keep tablets and blanks in bed under his pillow, that at leisure hours he might accustom his hand to form the letters; however, as he began his efforts late in life, and not at the proper time, he met with little success. . . . He cherished with the greatest fervor and devotion the principles of the Christian religion, which had been instilled in him from

* Einhard, *Vita Caroli Magni,* translated by S. E. Turner (New York, 1880) pp. 56-65, *passim.*

infancy. . . . He took great pains to improve the church
reading and singing, for he was well skilled in both, although he neither read in public nor sang, except in a low
tone with others. . . . He cared for the Church of St.
Peter the Apostle at Rome above all other holy and sacred
places, and heaped high its treasury with a vast wealth of
gold, silver, and precious stones.

— Reading No. 3 —

THE TREATY OF VERDUN, 843*

*The history of Germany begins properly with the
Treaty of Verdun, by which in 843 the Carolingian Empire
was divided among the three grandsons of Charlemagne.
The text of the treaty has not survived, but the following
account, attributed to Prudentius, Bishop of Troyes (845-
861), was found in the monastery of St. Bertin, near St.
Omer, Pas de Calais.*

✓   ✓   ✓

Charles went to confer with his brothers and met
them at Verdun. There the portions were distributed.
Louis obtained all the land beyond the Rhine and on this
side of the Rhine the cities and districts of Speyer, Worms,
and Mayence. Lothair received the country between the
Rhine and the mouth of the river Scheldt; thence south-
wards including the counties of Cambrai, Hainault,
Namur, Castritus and those counties, which are held to lie
immediately on this side of the Meuse, down to the con-
fluence of the Saône and the Rhône, and along the

---

* *Annales Bertiniani (Prudentii Trecensis)* in *Monumenta
    Germaniae Historica, Scriptores,* edited by George H.
    Pertz and others (120 vols., Hanover and Berlin, 1826-
    1925) I, 440.

Rhône to the sea with the counties adjoining it on either
side. All the other territories as far as Spain fell to
Charles. Then oaths were taken, and they went their
several ways.

— Reading No. 4 —

THE GOLDEN BULL, 1356*

*The central document of German constitutional history
in the Middle Ages, the Golden Bull of Charles IV remained the fundamental law of the Holy Roman Empire
until its dissolution in 1806. This document, in legalizing
the independence of the Electors and the powerlessness of
the Crown, epitomized the particularism that persisted
and divided the Germanies until the late nineteenth century.*

✓   ✓   ✓

I. 1. We decree and determine by this imperial edict
that, whenever the electoral princes are summoned according to the ancient and praiseworthy custom to meet and
elect a king of the Romans and future emperor, each one
of them shall be bound to furnish on demand an escort
and safe-conduct to his fellow electors or their representatives, within his own lands and as much farther as he can,
for the journey to and from the city where the election
is to be held. Any electoral prince who refuses to furnish
escort and safe-conduct shall be liable to the penalities for

* Wilhelm Altmann and Ernst Bernheim, *Ausgewählte Urkun-
    den zur Erläuterung der Verfassungsgeschichte Deutsch-
    lands im Mittelalter* (3rd ed., Berlin, 1904) pp. 54-83.
    Translated by Oliver J. Thatcher and Edgar H. McNeal,
    Source Book for Medieval History (New York, 1905)
    pp. 284-85, *passim.*

perjury and to the loss of his electoral vote for that occasion. . . .

16. When the news of the death of the king of the Romans has been received at Mayence, within one month from the date of receiving it the archbishop of Mayence shall send notices of the death and the approaching election to all the electoral princes. . . .

II. 2. OATH TAKEN BY THE ELECTORS: "I, archbishop of Mayence, archchancellor of the Empire of Germany, electoral prince, swear on the Holy Gospels here before me, and by the faith which I owe to God and to the Holy Roman Empire, that with the aid of God, and according to my best judgment and knowledge, I will cast my vote, in this election of the king of the Romans and future emperor, for a person fitted to rule the Christian people. I will give my voice and vote freely, uninfluenced by any agreement, price, bribe, promise, or anything of the sort, by whatever name it may be called. So help me God and all the saints." . . .

IV. 1. In the imperial diet, at the council-board, table, and all other places where the emperor or king of the Romans meets with the electoral princes, the seats shall be arranged as follows. On the right of the emperor, first, the archbishop of Mayence, or of Cologne, according to the province in which the meeting is held . . . ; second, the king of Bohemia, because he is a crowned and anointed prince; third, the count palatinate of the Rhine; on the left of the emperor, first the archbishop of Cologne, or of Mayence; second, the duke of Saxony. third, the margrave of Brandenburg.

2. When the imperial throne comes vacant, the archbishop of Mayence shall have the authority, which he has had from old, to call the other electors together for the election.

At the diet, the margrave of Brandenburg shall offer water to the emperor or king, to wash his hands; the king of Bohemia shall have the right to offer him the cup first, although, by reason of his royal dignity, he shall not be bound to do this unless he desires; the count palatine of the Rhine shall offer him food; and the duke of Saxony shall act as his marshal in the accustomed manner. . . .

— Reading No. 5 —

LUTHER'S NINETY-FIVE THESES, OCTOBER 31, 1517*

On October 31, 1517, the thirty-four-year-old Martin Luther posted his famous Ninety-Five Theses on the doors of the Schlosskirche at Wittenberg. This event marked the first great step in the rupture of the Church and gave the signal for the beginning of the Reformation. Extracts from the document follow.

✓   ✓   ✓

Disputation of Dr. Martin Luther Concerning Indulgences

In the desire and with the purpose of elucidating the truth, a disputation will be held on the underwritten propositions at Wittenberg, under the presidency of the Reverend Martin Luther, monk of the Order of St. Augustine, Master of Arts and Sacred Theology, and ordinary lecturer in the same at that place. He, therefore, asks those who cannot be present and discuss the subject with us orally to do so by letter in their absence. In the name of our Lord Jesus Christ. Amen.

1. Our Lord and Master Jesus Christ in saying "Repent ye" [*poenitentiam agite*], etc., intended that the whole life of believers should be penitence [*poenitentia*]. . . .

5. The Pope has neither the will nor the power to remit any penalities except those which he has imposed by his own authority, or by that of the canons. . . .

6. The Pope has no power to remit any guilt, except by declaring and warranting it to have been remitted by God; or at most by remitting cases reserved for himself; in which cases, if his power were despised, guilt would certainly remain.

* *Luthers Werke* (Erlangen, 1828-1870), translated and edited by H. Wace and C. A. Buckheim in *First Principles of the Reformation* (Philadelphia, 1885) pp. 6-14.

7. Certainly, God remits no man's guilt without at the same time subjecting him, humbled in all things, to the authority of his representative, the priest. . . .

27. They preach mad, who say that the soul flies out of purgatory as soon as the money thrown into the chest rattles.

28. It is certain that, when the money rattles in the chest, avarice and gain may be increased, but the suffrage of the Church depends on the will of God alone. . . .

32. Those who believe that, through letters of pardon, they are made sure of their own salvation, will be eternally damned along with their teachers.

33. We must especially beware of those who say that these Pardons from the Pope are that inestimable gift of God by which man is reconciled to God. . . .

50. Christians should be taught that, if the Pope were acquainted with the exactions of the preachers of pardons, he would prefer that the Basilica of St. Peter should be burnt to ashes, than that it should be built up with the skin, flesh, and bones of his sheep. . . .

56. The treasures of the Church, whence the Pope grants indulgences, are neither sufficiently named nor known among the peoples of Christ. . . .

75. To think that the Papal pardons have such power that they could absolve a man even if—by an impossibility—he had violated the Mother of God, is madness.

76. We affirm on the contrary that Papal pardons cannot take away even the least of venal sins, as regards its guilt. . . .

94. Christians should be exhorted to strive to follow Christ through pains, deaths, and hells.

95. And thus trust to enter heaven through many tribulations, rather than in the security of peace.

— Reading No. 6 —

FREDERICK THE GREAT ON THE DUTIES OF A PRINCE, 1781 *

In 1781 Frederick the Great of Prussia (1712-1786) wrote "An Essay on Forms of Government and on the Duties of Sovereigns," from which the extract below is taken.

The sovereign is attached by indissoluble ties to the body of the state; hence it follows that he, by repercussion, is sensible of all the ills which afflict his subjects; and the people, in like manner, suffer from the misfortunes which affect their sovereign. There is but one general good, which is that of the state. If the monarch lose his provinces, he is no longer able as formerly to assist his subjects. If misfortunes have obliged him to contract debts, they must be liquidated by the poor citizens; and, in return, if the people are not numerous, and if they are oppressed by poverty, the sovereign is destitute of all resource. These are truths so incontestable that there is no need to insist on them further.

I once more repeat, the sovereign represents the state; he and his people form but one body, which can only be happy as far as united by concord. The prince is to the nation he governs what the head is to the man; it is his duty to see, think, and act for the whole community, that he may procure it every advantage of which it is capable. If it be intended that a monarchical should excel a republican government, sentence is pronounced on the sovereign. He must be active, possess integrity, and collect his whole powers, that he may be able to run the career he has commenced. . . .

* *Posthumous Works of Frederic II, King of Prussia,* edited by J. Holcroft (London, 1789) pp. 14-16.

— Reading No. 7 —

DISSOLUTION OF THE HOLY ROMAN EMPIRE, AUGUST 6, 1806*

On July 12, 1806, Napoleon set up the Confederation of the Rhine "forever separated from the territory of the Germanic Empire," and on August 1 sent a brusque message to the Imperial Diet announcing the end of the Holy Roman Empire. Five days later Francis II abdicated as Holy Roman Emperor, but retained the title of Francis I, Emperor of Austria.

Thus the old Holy Roman Empire, which had been the only bond linking the Germanies together for more than eight hundred years since the imperial coronation by the pope of Otto I in 962, disappeared, and the legal existence of the German states that had grown up on its territory was recognized. This consolidation of the Germanies survived Napoleon's downfall, and paved the way for Germany's national unification.

✓   ✓   ✓

A

Napoleon's Note to the Imperial Diet, August 1, 1806

The undersigned, *chargé d'affaires* of His Majesty the Emperor of the French and King of Italy at the Diet of the German Empire, has been ordered by His Majesty to make the following declaration to the Diet:

Their Majesties the Kings of Bavaria and of Württemberg, the Sovereign Princes of Regensburg, Baden,

* A. J. H. and Jules de Clercq, *Receuil des traités de la France, publié sous les auspices du ministère des affaires étrangères* (Paris, 1864-1917) II, 183-84; *Moniteur,* August 14 1806.

Berg, Hesse-Darmstadt and Nassau, and the other leading Princes of the south and west of Germany have resolved to form a confederation among themselves which shall protect them against future emergencies. They have thus ceased to be States of the Empire.

The Diet no longer has a will of its own. The judgments of the superior law courts can no longer be executed. There is such serious weakness that the federal bond no longer gives any protection and only means a source of dissension and discord between the powers. . . .

His Majesty the Emperor and King is, therefore, compelled to state that he can no longer recognize the existence of the German Constitution. He acknowledges, however, the complete and absolute sovereignty of each of the Princes whose States compose Germany today, and maintains with them the same relations as with the other independent Powers of Europe.

His Majesty the Emperor and King has accepted the title: *Protector of the Confederation of the Rhine*. He has been motivated solely by the interests of peace, so that by his constant mediation between the weak and the powerful he may avoid every kind of disorder and dissension. . . .

Regensburg, August 1, 1806.

BACHER

B

Abdication of Francis II, August 6, 1806

We, Francis the Second, by the Grace of God Roman Emperor Elect, Ever August, Hereditary Emperor of Austria, etc., King of Germany, Hungary, Bohemia, Croatia, Dalmatia, Slavonia, Galizia, Lodomeria and Jerusalem, Archduke of Austria, etc.

Since the Peace of Pressburg all our care and attention has been directed to the purpose of fulfilling carefully all the provisions of the said treaty, as well as the preservation of peace so necessary to the happiness of our subjects, and the strengthening in every way of the friendly relations now so happily established. We could but await the outcome of events in order to decide whether the significant changes in the German Empire resulting from the peace terms would permit us to fulfill the weighty duties which devolve upon us as head of the Empire. But the results of certain articles of the Treaty of Petersburg . . . have convinced us that it would be impossible under these circumstances further to fulfill the duties which we have assumed by the conditions of our election. . . .

We proclaim, therefore, that we consider the ties which have thus far united us to the German Empire as dissolved; that we look upon the office and dignity of the Imperial headship as dissolved by the formation of a separate federation of the Rhenish States, and regard ourselves as freed from all obligations to the German Empire. Herewith we lay down the Imperial crown which is associated with such obligations and we relinquish the Imperial Government which we have thus far conducted. . . .

Done at our capital and royal residence, Vienna, August 6, 1806, in the 15th year of our reign as Emperor and hereditary ruler of the Austrian lands.

FRANCIS

— Reading No. 8 —

THE PRUSSIAN REFORM EDICT OF OCTOBER 9, 1807*

The legislative reforms carried out in Prussia in 1807-8 were to some extent similar to the Napoleonic reforms. The following edict of Frederick William III was concerned with the land problem.

✓   ✓   ✓

WE, FREDERICK WILLIAM, BY THE GRACE OF GOD KING OF PRUSSIA, ETC.

Hereby make known and proclaim that:

Since the establishment of peace, we have been

* G. H. Pertz, *Das Leben des Ministers Freiherrn vom Stein* (Berlin, 1850) II, 23 ff.

concerned above all with the care for the depressed condition of our loyal subjects and with the quickest possible
revival and greatest possible improvement of the situation.
We have considered that because of the widespread want,
the means at our disposal would not be sufficient to assist
each individual, and even if they were sufficient, we could
not hope to accomplish our purpose. Moreover, in accordance with the imperative demands of justice and with
the principles of a wise economic policy, we should like
to remove every obstacle which in the past has prevented
the individual from attaining that prosperity he was capable of reaching. . . . It is our desire, therefore, to reduce
restrictions [on ownership of land and status of the
agricultural worker] so far as the common welfare demands. Therefore, we proclaim the following:

#1. FREEDOM OF EXCHANGE OF PROPERTY. Every
inhabitant of our States shall have the right, without any
limitation upon the part of the State, to own or mortgage
landed property of any kind. It follows that the noble,
therefore, may own not only noble, but also non-noble,
citizen, or peasant lands of any kind, and the citizen and
peasant may own not only citizen, peasant, or other non-
noble, but also noble tracts of land without the necessity,
in any case, of acquiring special permission for any
acquisition whatsoever. . . .

#2. FREE CHOICE OF OCCUPATION. Every noble
is allowed, from this time on, without any derogation
from his status, to engage in citizen occupation, while
every citizen is permitted to pass from the citizen into the
peasant class or vice versa. . . .

#12. From Martinmas, 1810, all serfdom shall
end throughout our entire realm. From Martinmas, 1810,
there shall be only free individuals, such as is already
the case on the royal domains in all our provinces—
free persons, but still subject, as a matter of
course, to all the obligations which bind them, as free
persons, because of the ownership of an estate or because
of a special contract.

Every one whom it may concern, especially our
provincial authorities and other officials, is required to
conform exactly and loyally to this declaration of our
supreme will, and this ordinance is to be made universally known.

Given under our royal signature, at Memel, October 9, 1807.

FREDERICK WILLIAM [III]

SCHRÖTTER STEIN SCHRÖTTER II

— Reading No. 9 —

POETRY OF THE WAR OF LIBERATION, 1812-1813*

German romanticism attained its full development during the Napoleonic period with Fichte, Schleiermacher, Novalis, Görres, Tieck, the Schlegel brothers, Schenkendorf, Arndt, and Körner. Following are several stanzas from "Prayer During Battle," by Theodor Körner, whose death in the War of Liberation made him a popular hero.

✦ ✦ ✦

PRAYER DURING BATTLE

Father I call on thee!
Roaring the cannons hurl round me their clouds,
Flashing the lightning bursts wildly its shrouds.
  God of battles, I call upon thee!
  Father, O guide thou me!

.Father, O guide thou me!
Lead me to victory, lead me to death!
Lord, I'll acknowledge thee with my last breath.
  Lord, as thou listest, guide thou me!
  God, I acknowledge thee! . . .

  Father, I honour thee!
'Tis not a fight for this world's golden hoard;

* Alfred Baskerville, *The Poetry of Germany* (4th ed., Baden-Baden and Hamburg, 1876) pp. 225-26.

Holy is what we protect with the sword,
    Hence falling, or vanquishing, praise be to thee!
        God, I submit to thee!

        God, I submit to thee!
When round me roar the dread thunders of death,
When my veins' torrent shall drain my last breath;
        Then, O my God, I submit to thee!
            Father, I call on thee!

— Reading No. 10 —

THE CARLSBAD DECREES, SEPTEMBER 1, 1819*

The Carlsbad Decrees, instituted by Metternich as a means of holding the German Confederation under Austrian domination, suppressed liberty in the Germanies for a full generation. Below are extracts from the decrees.

✦   ✦   ✦

1. There shall be appointed for each university a special representative of the ruler of each State, the said representatives to have appropriate instructions and extended powers, and they shall have their place of residence where the university is located. . . .

This representative shall enforce strictly the existing laws and disciplinary regulations; he shall observe with care the attitude shown by the university instructors in their public lectures and registered courses; and he shall, without directly interfering in scientific matters or in teaching methods, give a beneficial direction to the teaching, keeping in view the future attitude of the students. Finally, he shall give unceasing attention to every-

* P. A. G. von Meyer, *Corpus juris confoederationis Germanicae* (Frankfort-on-Main, 1833) II, 138 ff.

thing that may promote morality . . . among the students. . . .

2. The confederated governments mutually pledge themselves to eliminate from the universities or any other public institutions all instructors who shall have obviously proven their unfitness for the important work entrusted to them by openly deviating from their duties, or by going beyond the boundaries of their functions, or by abusing their legitimate influence over young minds, or by presenting harmful ideas hostile to public order or subverting existing governmental instructions. . . .

3. The laws that for some time have been directed against secret and unauthorized societies in the universities shall be strictly enforced. Such laws are applicable especially to the association formed some years ago under the name of *Allgemeine Burschenschaft,* for the organization of that society implies the completely impermissible idea of permanent fellowship and constant inter-communication between the universities. . . .

4. No student who shall have been expelled from any university by virtue of a decision of the University Senate ratified or initiated by the special representative of the Government, shall be admitted by any other university.

— Reading No. 11 —

INTERNATIONAL TREATY GUARANTEEING THE NEUTRALITY OF BELGIUM, APRIL 19, 1839*

At London on April 19, 1839, a treaty was signed between Great Britain, Austria, France, Prussia, and Russia, on the one part, and The Netherlands, on the other, in which the union between Holland and Belgium, estab-

* E. Hertslet, ed., *The Map of Europe by Treaty* (London, 1875) II, 982-85.

*lished at Vienna in 1815, was formally dissolved. A
similar treaty was signed with Belgium. In the annex to
the first treaty, and repeated in the second, was an
article that guaranteed the independence and neutrality
of Belgium. This guarantee was re-stated in a treaty between Great Britain and Prussia signed at London, on
August 9, 1870. The "scrap of paper," signed by Palmerston, Senff, Sebastiani, Bülow, and di Borgo in 1839, is
reproduced here.*

> *Annex to the Treaty signed at London,
> on the 19th of April 1839, between
> Great Britain, Austria, France, Prus-
> sia, and Russia, on the one part, and
> the Netherlands, on the other part*

ARTICLE 1. The Belgian Territory shall be composed
of the Provinces of: South Brabant; Liege; Namur;
Hainault; West Flanders; East Flanders; Antwerp; and
Limburg; such as they formed part of the United Kingdom of the Netherlands in 1815, with the exception of
those districts of the Province of Limburg which are
designated in Article 4.

The Belgian Territory shall, moreover, comprise that
part of the Grand Duchy of Luxemburg which is specified in Article 2.

ARTICLE 2. In the Grand Duchy of Luxemburg, the
limits of the Belgian Territory shall be such as will hereinafter be described. . . .

ARTICLE 4. In execution of that part of Article I which
relates to the Province of Limburg, and in consequence
of the cessions which His Majesty the King of the Netherlands, Grand Duke of Luxemburg, makes in Article 2,
His said Majesty shall possess, either to be held by him
in his character of Grand Duke of Luxemburg, or for
the purpose of being united to Holland, those Territories,
the limits of which are hereinafter described. . . .

ARTICLE 7. Belgium, within the limits specified in
Articles 1, 2, and 4, shall form an Independent and per-
petually Neutral State. It shall be bound to observe such
Neutrality towards all other States. . . .

— Reading No. 12 —

FREDERICK WILLIAM IV'S REFUSAL OF THE IMPERIAL CROWN, MAY 15, 1849 *

On March 28, 1849, the Frankfort Assembly offered "the hereditary imperial dignity" to Frederick William IV of Prussia. Following are excerpts from an imperial proclamation refusing the offer.

✓   ✓   ✓

TO MY PEOPLE!

Using the pretense that they are working in the interests of Germany, the enemies of the Fatherland have raised high the standard of revolt, first in neighboring Saxony, and then in several districts of South Germany. . . .

I was not able to submit a favorable reply to the offer of a crown by the German National Assembly, because that body does not have the right, without the consent of the German Governments, to bestow the crown they have offered me, and, in addition, because they tendered the crown upon the condition that I would accept a constitution which could not be reconciled with the rights and safety of the German States. . . .

A party now dominating the Assembly is in league with the terrorists. While they urge the unity of Germany as a pretense, they are really fighting the battle of godlessness, perjury, and theft, and arousing a war. . . .

While such crimes have put an end to the hope that the Frankfort Assembly can achieve German unity, I have, with a fidelity and persistence suitable to my royal position, never given up hope. My Government has taken

* M. Schilling, *Quellenbuch zur Geschichte der Neuzeit* (Berlin, 1890) p. 431.

up with the more important German States the work on the German constitution begun by the Frankfort Assembly.

That is my method. Only madness or deception can dare, in view of these facts, to maintain that I have given up the cause of German unity, or that I am untrue to my earliest convictions and promises. . . .

Charlottenburg, May 15, 1849   FREDERICK WILLIAM

— Reading No. 13 —

BISMARCK'S "IRON AND BLOOD" SPEECH, SEPTEMBER 30, 1862*

On September 30, 1862, Bismarck appeared before the Budget Commission of the Lower House of the Prussian Parliament and attempted to persuade it to appropriate army increases desired by William I. One phrase from this famous speech, with its rhythm changed from "iron and blood" to "blood and iron," gave clear indication of Germany's future course.

✓   ✓   ✓

Germany looks not to Prussia's liberalism but to her power. Bavaria, Württemberg, and Baden may indulge in liberalism, but no person will because of that reason assign Prussia's role to them. Prussia must gather up her strength and maintain it in readiness for the opportune moment, which already has passed by several times. Since the Treaty of Vienna, Prussia's borders have not been favorable for a healthy state life. Not by parliamentary speeches and majority votes are the great questions of the day determined—that was the great mistake of 1848 and 1849—but by iron and blood.

* J. Hohfeld, *Deutsche Reichsgeschichte in Dokumenten* (Berlin, 1927) I. Halbband, p. 27.

— Reading No. 14 —

GERMAN SCIENCE AND THE NEW INDUSTRIAL REVOLUTION, 1865 *

At a meeting of natural scientists and physicians held at Hanover on September 20, 1865, the eminent pathologist and politician Rudolf Virchow (1821-1902) delivered an address titled "On the National Development and the Importance of the Natural Sciences." In this important speech, from which extracts are given below, the great pathologist, who had been directing a constant stream of original research work at the Pathological Institute in Berlin, placed the achievements of German science on a national basis. It was an expression of the steadily intensifying nationalism which penetrated into all branches of German national life.

✓   ✓   ✓

*Extracts from a speech by Rudolf Virchow before a meeting of German natural scientists and physicians, September 20, 1865 **

Gentlemen! When we recall how many times we have assembled, when we think about how our hearts have been drawn closer together over the years, how differences among us in scientific life as in everyday life have gradually become reconciled, I must say, considering the importance of science and natural science, that there can be no doubt that these meetings have great national importance. They are valuable because they represent

* Rudolf Virchow, *Über die nationale Entwickelung und Bedeutung der Naturwissenschaften,* quoted in Theodor Flathe, ed., *Deutsche Reden: Denkmäler zur vaterländischen Geschichte des neunzehnten Jahrhunderts* (2 vols., Leipzig, 1893) I, 612-27, *passim.*

the united work and the common activity of all, even of those who are widely separated. . . .

When we realize what our people have accomplished in the way of spiritual capital since the Reformation—indeed, when we weigh what has been done in a century in comparison with many preceding centuries—then the most enthusiastic proponents of Romanism and Latinism must agree that the degree to which the forms of learning have become national, as scientific knowledge became an ever larger ingredient in the national sum of knowledge, has resulted not merely in values practical and fruitful for the welfare of the people and prosperity of the State, but has also won more and more influence on general thinking, which, in its turn, has fruitfully affected scholarly research. . . .

Gentlemen! For thirty years these meetings of natural scientists have helped prepare the nation for what is now presented in our gatherings of political scientists. What we now call our system of political economy is, in my opinion, nothing more than natural science directed to the problem of the immediate life of the people. For me the meetings of the political economists are nothing more than another side of our own gatherings. . . .

I have never concerned myself with prophecies; I am more accustomed to make prognoses on the basis of precise experimentation in matters of health and sickness. That is also the way I look at the life of our nation. When I think about the development not only of natural science but also the branches which are bound to it, in industry, techniques, and the ordinary life of the handworker, as well as in scholarly research in statistics, political economy, and political science, and how all this tends more and more to show the unity of knowledge, . . . then, I believe, we can depend upon the fact that the national importance which natural science has won for itself during the last fifty years promises to give greater results of unparalleled magnificence in the next fifty years. . . .

— Reading No. 15 —

PROCLAMATION OPENING THE AUSTRO-PRUSSIAN WAR, JUNE 18, 1866*

Bismarck utilized the quarrel over Schleswig-Holstein as a means of challenging the hegemony of Austria-Hungary in Central European affairs. On June 18, 1866, King William I issued the following proclamation opening the Austro-Prussian War.

✓   ✓   ✓

. . . The fault is not mine should my people have hard battles to fight and mayhap heavy burdens to bear. There is no alternative left to us. We must struggle for our very existence. It is necessary that we engage in a life-and-death struggle with those who would cast down the Prussia of the Great Elector, of Frederick the Great, the Prussia which emerged triumphant from the War of Liberation, from the position to which the skill and strength of her princes and the bravery, loyalty, and character of her people have raised her.

Let us pray to Almighty God, the director of the history of all nations, the disposer of battles, to bless our arms. Should he give us victory, then we shall be strong enough to renew, in a firmer and more beneficent manner, the bonds which have loosely bound the German lands together, in name rather than in fact, and which have now been torn apart by those who fear the right and might of the national spirit.

May God be with us!

BERLIN, JUNE 18, 1866   WILLIAM

* Extracted from the text in Erick Eyck, *Bismarck and the German Empire* (London, 1950) p. 127.

— Reading No. 16 —

THE PRUSSIAN BILL OF INDEMNITY, SEPTEMBER 14, 1866*

On September 1, 1866, Bismarck appeared before the Prussian Landtag and, in a witty mood, asked for a bill of indemnity retroactively legalizing his actions in ruling unconstitutionally from 1862 to 1866. He expressed no regrets, but merely asked for a bill righting the wrong he had done. The indemnification was voted by a large majority.

✔   ✔   ✔

ARTICLE 1. The present law shall serve as an annex to the subjoining summary of the State's income and expenditure for the years 1862, 1863, 1864, and 1865 instead of the constitutional and annual accounting for each fiscal year, as a basis for the accounting and release of the State Administration.

ARTICLE 2. The State Administration grants indemnity with regard to the lawfully established and in due course publicized State budget, with the exception of the resolution of the Landtag on the release of the State Administration from proposal of a yearly accounting, to such a degree, that it, considering the responsibility of the State Administration, shall be held as if the stewardship had been managed in the above-mentioned time on the basis of a State budget lawfully established and in due course publicized.

ARTICLE 3. The State Administration is hereby empowered to expand a sum up to 154 million talers for the year 1866.

ARTICLE 4. The State Administration is bound to place before the Landtag an accounting of the State income and expenditures for the year 1866-1867.

* *Das Staatsarchiv* (Hamburg, 1866) Vol. 11, No. 2398, pp. 287 ff.

— Reading No. 17 —

THE EMS DISPATCH, JULY 13, 1870*

Below are the original text of the Ems Dispatch as sent by Heinrich Abeken, German Councillor of Legation at Paris, to Bismarck on July 13, 1870, and the revised version which the latter submitted to the press. In its abbreviated form the dispatch gave the impression of an ultimatum. Both the French and German people interpreted it as an insult. France declared war on Prussia on July 19th.

✓   ✓   ✓

The Abeken Text

EMS, JULY 13, 1870.
TO THE FEDERAL CHAN-CELLOR, COUNT BISMARCK, No. 27, No. 61 EOD. 3:10 P.M. (STATION EMS: RUSH!) His Majesty the King writes to me:

"M. Benedetti intercepted me on the Promenade in order to demand ot me most insistently that I should authorize him to telegraph immediately to Paris that I shall obligate myself for all future time never again to give my approval to the candidacy of the Hohenzollerns should it be renewed. I refused to agree to this, the last time somewhat severely, informing him that one dare not and cannot

Bismarck's Edited Version

After the reports of the renunciation by the hereditary Prince of Hohenzollern had been officially transmitted by the Royal Government of Spain to the Imperial Government of France, the French Ambassador presented to His Majesty the King at Ems the demand to authorize him to telegraph to Paris that His Majesty the King would obligate himself for all future time never again to give his approval to the candidacy of the Hohenzollerns should it be renewed.

* *Propyläen Weltgeschichte* (Berlin, 1930) VIII, 248.

Abeken Text (cont.)   *Bismarck Version (cont.)*

assume such obligations *à tout jamais*. Naturally, I informed him that I had received no news as yet, and since he had been informed earlier than I by way of Paris and Madrid he could easily understand that my Government was once again out of the matter."

Since then His Majesty has received a dispatch from the Prince [Charles Anthony]. As His Majesty informed Count Benedetti that he was expecting news from the Prince, His Majesty himself, in view of the above-mentioned demand and in consonance with the advice of Count Eulenburg and myself, decided not to receive the French envoy again but to inform him through an adjutant that His Majesty had now received from the Prince confirmation of the news which Benedetti had already received from Paris, and that he had nothing further to say to the Ambassador. His Majesty leaves it to the judgment of Your Excellency whether or not to communicate at once the new demand by Benedetti and its rejection to our ambassadors and to the press.

[Signed] A[beken] 13.7.70

His Majesty the King thereupon refused to receive the French envoy again and informed him through an adjutant that His Majesty has nothing further to say to the Ambassador.

— Reading No. 18 —

THE SURRENDER OF NAPOLEON III, SEPTEMBER 1, 1870*

In the following exchange of messages Napoleon III surrendered to King William I of Prussia after the defeat at Sedan.

✔   ✔   ✔

Napoleon to King William

Sir, my brother!

Not having been able to die in the midst of my troops, it only remains for me to surrender my sword to the hands of Your Majesty.

I am, Your Majesty's good brother

Sedan, September 1, 1870   NAPOLEON

King William's Reply

Sir, my brother!

While regretting the circumstances in which we shall meet, I accept the sword of Your Majesty, and I urge you to grant one of your officers full power to arrange the capitulation of the army that has fought so bravely under your orders. On my side, I have designated General Moltke to that effect.

I am Your Majesty's

Good Brother,

Before Sedan, September 1, 1870   WILLIAM

* *Der deutsch-französische Krieg,* War Historical Division of the Great General Staff (Berlin, 1872-1881) Part 1, Section 8, p. 313.

— Reading No. 19 —

PROCLAMATION OF THE SECOND GERMAN REICH, JANUARY 18, 1871 *

The second German Reich came into being on January 18, 1871, the handiwork of Bismarck and the product of three wars. Following is William I's proclamation announcing the restoration of the German imperial office.

✔   ✔   ✔

Whereas the German princes and the free cities have unanimously called upon us to renew and to assume, with the restoration of the German Empire, the German imperial office, which has been empty for more than sixty years; and

Whereas adequate arrangements have been provided for this in the constitution of the German Confederation;

We, William, by the grace of God King of Prussia, do herewith declare that we have considered it a duty to our common fatherland to answer the summons of the united German princes and cities and to accept the German imperial title. In consequence, we and our successors on the throne of Prussia will henceforth bear the imperial title in all our relations and in all the business of the German Empire, and we hope to God that the German nation will be granted the ability to fashion a propitious future for the fatherland under the symbol of its ancient glory. We assume the imperial title, conscious of the duty of protecting, with German loyalty, the rights of the Empire and of its members, of keeping the peace, and of protecting the independence of Germany, which depends

* Horst Kohl, ed., *Die politische Reden des Fürsten von Bismarck; historische-kritische Gesammtausgabe* (14 vols., Stuttgart, 1892-1904) IV, 444.

in its turn upon the united strength of the people. We assume the title in the hope that the German people will be granted the ability to enjoy the reward of its ardent and self-sacrificing wars in lasting peace, within boundaries which afford the fatherland a security against renewed French aggression which has been lost for centuries. And may God grant that we and our successors on the imperial throne may at all times increase the wealth of the German Empire, not by military conquests, but by the blessings and the gifts of peace, in the realm of national prosperity, liberty, and morality.

Issued at general headquarters, Versailles, Jan. 18, 1871.   WILLIAM [I]

— Reading No. 20 —

CONSTITUTION OF THE SECOND GERMAN REICH, APRIL 16, 1871*

The Constitution of the new German Empire provided for a federal union of twenty-five states, but in effect it set up a semi-autocratic state ruled by the King of Prussia, the Chancellor, and Prussian Junkers and officials. Following are extracts from the Constitution.

✓   ✓   ✓

1. Federal Territory

ARTICLE 1. The Federal territory consists of the States of Prussia (with Lauenburg), Bavaria, Saxony, Württemberg, Baden, Hesse, Mecklenburg-Schwerin, Saxe-Weimar, Mecklenburg-Strelitz, Oldenburg, Brunswick, Saxe-Meinigen, Saxe-Altenburg, Saxe-Coburg-Gotha, Anhalt, Schwarzburg-Rudolstadt, Schwarzburg-Sonderhausen,

* Translated from the official German version, 22d ed. (Leipzig, 1920) *passim*.

Waldeck, Reuss of the Elder Line, Reuss of the Younger Line, Schaumburg-Lippe, Lippe, Lübeck, Bremen, and Hamburg.

2. *Imperial Legislation*

ARTICLE 2. The Empire exercises the right of legislation within the Federal territory according to the provisions of the Constitution, and with the effect that Imperial legislation shall take precedence over State legislation. Imperial legislation holds its binding force through proclamations by the Reich in its Imperial Legislative journal [*Reichsgesetzblatt*]. . . .

3. *Bundesrat*

ARTICLE 7. The Bundesrat shall decide upon:

1. Proposals made by the Reichstag and decisions made by it;

2. The implementation of the general administrative measures and orders necessitated by Imperial legislation, in so far as Imperial legislation has not determined otherwise;

3. The correction of deficiencies that arise in the implementation of the above-mentioned regulations. . . .

ARTICLE 8. The Bundesrat shall organize from its membership permanent committees for (1) the Army and its citadels, (2) the Navy, (3) customs and taxes, (4) trade and communications, (5) railroads, post, and telegraph, (6) judiciary, and (7) accounts. . . .

4. *Presiding Officer*

ARTICLE 11. The Presiding Officer of the Federation shall be the King of Prussia, who shall bear the name German Emperor. The Emperor shall represent the Empire in the Law of Nations, to declare war and conclude peace in the name of the Empire, to enter into alliances and other treaties with foreign States, and to accredit and receive ambassadors. . . .

5. *Reichstag*

ARTICLE 20. The Reichstag shall be elected by universal and direct elections with secret voting.

ARTICLE 21. Public officials are not permitted vacations in order to serve in the Reichstag. . . .

ARTICLE 22. The meetings of the Reichstag shall be public. . . .

ARTICLE 23. The Reichstag shall have the right, within the competence of Imperial legislation, to present and to pass on petitions directed to it to the Bundesrat and the Imperial Chancellor.

ARTICLE 24. The legislative period of the Reichstag lasts five years. For the dissolution of the Reichstag during this period a resolution of the Bundesrat with the concurrence of the Emperor is required. . . .

ARTICLE 28. The Reichstag acts with an absolute majority. The presence of a majority of the legal number of members is required for the validity of its actions. . . .

6. *Customs and Trade Systems*

ARTICLE 33. Germany shall constitute a customs and trade territory surrounded by a common customs barrier. Excluded are those individual territories which because of their situation are not suitable for inclusion within the customs lines. . . .

7. *Railway System*

ARTICLE 41. Railroads which are regarded as necessary in the interest of the defense of Germany or in the interest of common traffic may be operated by the Empire or given as concessions to private enterprise, with rights of expropriation guarded, provided that imperial legislation for this purpose, without prejudice to the State administrations, has been passed and agreed to by the Federal States whose territory is used by the railroads. . . .

8. *Postal and Telegraph Systems*

ARTICLE 48. The postal and telegraph systems shall be established and controlled for the entire territory of the German Reich as a unified state system of communication. . . .

9. *Navy and Merchant Marine*

ARTICLE 53. The Navy of the Empire shall be unified under the high command of the Emperor. The organization and construction of the Navy shall be the responsibility of the Emperor, who shall name the officers and officials of the Navy, and to whom the officers, officials, and crews shall take their oath. . . .

ARTICLE 54. The commercial ships of all federal States shall form a unified merchant marine. . . .

ARTICLE 55. The flag of the Navy and merchant marine shall be black, white, and red.

10. Consular Affairs

ARTICLE 56. The entire system of consulates of the German Empire shall be under the supervision of the Emperor, who shall install all consuls upon recommendation of the Committee of the Bundesrat for Trade and Communication.

No State consuls can function within the official districts of the German consuls. . . .

11. Imperial War Department

ARTICLE 57. Every German is subject to military service and shall not be represented by a substitute in the performance of this duty.

ARTICLE 58. The costs and charges of the entire War Department of the Empire and of all the Federal States shall be borne in common. . . .

ARTICLE 59. Every German subject to military service shall serve in the standing army for seven years, as a rule from his completed twentieth year to the beginning of his twenty-eighth year. . . .

12. Imperial Finances

ARTICLE 69. The income and expenditures of the Empire shall be stated annually and shall be announced in the budget of the Empire. . . .

ARTICLE 72. The Imperial Chancellor shall inform the *Bundesrat* and the *Reichstag* annually concerning the use of all income of the Empire. . . .

14. General Clauses

ARTICLE 78. Amendments of the Constitution are made by way of legislation. They shall be considered rejected if they have fourteen votes against them in the Bundesrat.

Those provisions of the Imperial Constitution, by which certain rights of individual members of the Federation in their relations to the whole are determined, can be amended only with the consent of the member of the Federation entitled to said rights.

— Reading No. 21 —

THE PEACE OF FRANKFORT, MAY 10, 1871*

Below are extracts from the Peace of Frankfort, which introduced a new epoch in the history of Germany. A tremendous indemnity was imposed on France, which, in addition to the loss of Alsace and Lorraine, stimulated a call for a revanche. The proud French could not forget defeat nor abstain from re-arming for retaliation.

✓   ✓   ✓

ARTICLE 7. The payment of one hundred millions [*francs*] shall take place in the thirty days which follow the re-establishment of the authority of the French Government in the city of Paris. One billion shall be paid during the course of the year and a half billion by the 1st of May, 1872. The three final billions shall be payable on the 2nd of March, 1874, as has been stipulated by the preliminary peace treaty. After the 2nd of March of the following year, the interest on these three billions of francs shall be paid each year, on the 3rd of March, at the rate of 5% per year. . . .

After the payment of the first half-billion and the ratification of the definite treaty of peace, the Departments of the Somme, the Lower Seine, and the Eure shall be evacuated in so far as they are still occupied by German troops. . . .

In all cases, that evacuation shall take place at the time of the payment of the third half-billion.

ARTICLE 8. The German troops will continue to refrain from taking requisitions from the land or in money from the occupied territories. . . .

* *Der deutsch-französische Krieg,* The War Historical Division of the Great General Staff (Berlin, 1872-1881) Part 2, Section 20, pp. 799 ff.

ARTICLE 10. The German Government, in understanding with the French Government, shall continue to return prisoners of war. The French Government, on their part, shall return those of the prisoners who are ready to be exchanged. . . . It is understood that the army of Paris and Versailles, after the establishment of the authority of the French Government in Paris and until the evacuation of the forts by German troops, shall not exceed 24,000 men. . . .

ARTICLE 11. All expelled Germans shall keep full and entire possession of all the property they have acquired in France. . . .

Done at Frankfort, May 10, 1871.

   (*Signed*) V. BISMARCK (*Signed*) JULES FAVRE
         ARNIM   POUYER-QUERTIER
                              E. DE GOULARD

— Reading No. 22 —

THE *KULTURKAMPF:* EXPULSION OF THE JESUITS, JULY 4, 1872*

Once the national unification of Germany was completed, Bismarck decided to settle matters with the Papacy, which he regarded as interfering in internal German affairs. His decree expelling the Jesuits from Germany, the text of which follows, marked the beginning of the so-called Kulturkampf (*struggle for civilization*), *1872-1878.*

       ✓   ✓   ✓

§1. The Order of the Society of Jesus and the orders relating to it, as well as the other similar order-like Congregations are debarred hereby from the territory of the German Reich.

* *Reichsgesetzblatt,* 1872, p. 253.

The formation of such establishments shall be dissolved within a period of time set by the Bundesrat, which
shall not be longer than six months.

§2. The members of the order of the Society of Jesus
or orders related to it or the similar order-like Congregations may be banished, if they are foreigners, from the
territory of the Confederation; if they are native to it,
their residence in certain districts or places may be
denied or they may be banished.

§3. The necessary regulations for the implementation
and execution of this law shall be proclaimed by the
Bundesrat.

Given at Bad Ems, July 4, 1872.

> (*L.S.*) WILLIAM
> PRINCE VON BISMARK

— Reading No. 23 —

THE ANTI-SOCIALIST LAW, OCTOBER 21, 1878 *

*Following his unsuccessful attack on the Catholic
Church in the* Kulturkampf, *Bismarck turned on the
Socialists—from "the black to the red international."
His opportunity came in 1878, when two attempts were
made on the life of the venerable William I by men who
were accused of being Socialists. Following is the text
of the Anti-Socialist Law of 1878.*

✓   ✓   ✓

§1. Organizations which through Social Democratic,
Socialist, or Communist activities aim to overthrow the
established State or social order are hereby forbidden.

The same ban holds for organizations in which Social
Democratic, Socialist, or Communist influence appears

* *Das Staatsarchiv,* 1878, Vol. 34, No. 6797, pp. 45 ff.

to be dedicated to the overthrow of the established State or social order, by breach of the public peace and especially by endangering the harmony of the classes.

Such organizations include fraternities of all kinds. . . .

§3. Independent trade unions (not registered) which, according to their statutes, aim for mutual benefits for their members are, for the time being, not to be banned, but are to be placed under special State control. . . .

Such assemblies include public festivals and parades. . . .

§11. All publications in which Social Democratic, Socialist, or Communist influence appears to be dedicated to the overthrow of the established State or social order by breach of the public peace, especially by endangering the harmony of the classes, are forbidden.

This ban on periodicals extends to all past issues, as soon as, on the basis of this law, one single issue is forbidden. . . .

§16. The collection of contributions on demand by Social Democratic, Socialist, or Communist organizations for the purpose of overthrowing the established State or social order, as well as public demands for payment of such contributions, are contrary to police regulations. This ban will be made public.

Complaints may be made only before the board of control.

§17. Anyone who takes part as a member in a forbidden organization, or anyone who exercises any activity in the interests of such an organization, shall be punished with a fine up to 500 marks or with imprisonment of three months. . . .

§30. This law goes into effect on the day of its proclamation and remains in effect until March 31, 1881.

— Reading No. 24 —

THE IDEALS OF HEINRICH VON TREITSCHKE*

One of the most influential figures in late-nineteenth-century German intellectual history was Heinrich von Treitschke (1834-1896), Professor of History at the University of Berlin. "A thousand times more patriot than professor," Treitschke expressed ideals which came to be accepted widely in Bismarckian and Wilhelmian Germany. Abstracted below are basic themes from his two major works.

On the State

In the State it is not only the great primitive forces of human nature that come into play; the State is the basis of all national life. Briefly, it may be affirmed that a State which is not capable of forming and maintaining an external organization of its civilizing activities deserves to perish.

On Aristocracy

Aristocracy . . . is a law of nature. . . . Every society, by its very nature, produces an aristocracy. . . .

The masses will always remain the masses. There can be no culture without its servants.

* Heinrich von Treitschke, *Die Politik*, edited by Max Cornelius (2d ed., 2 vols., Leipzig, 1899-1900) I, paragraph 3; 1, paragraph 2; I, 62-63; I, 50-52; II, 52-54; II, 360-61; I, 124; I, paragraph 3; I, 76. Heinrich von Treitschke, *Deutsche Geschichte im Neunzehnten Jahrhundert* (5 vols.; Leipzig, 1897-1904, V, 480.

On Monarchy

Monarchy is natural . . . and makes an appeal to the popular understanding. We Germans had an experience of this in the first years of our new Empire. How wonderfully the idea of a united Fatherland was embodied for us in the person of the venerable Emperor! How much it means to us that we can feel once more: That man is Germany: there is no gainsaying it!

On War

A thousand touching portraits testify to the sacred power of the love which a righteous war awakes in noble nations.

God will see to it that war always recurs as a drastic medicine for the human race.

War is elevating, because the individual disappears before the great conception of the State. The devotion of members of a community to each other is nowhere so splendidly conspicuous as in war.

On the Jews

The international Jew, hidden by the mask of different nationalities, is a disintegrative influence. He is of no further use to the world.

It is necessary to speak openly about the Jew, undisturbed by the fact that the Jewish press befouls what is purely historical truth.

On the British

The hypocritical English people, with the Bible in one hand and a pipe of opium in the other, possess no redeeming qualities.

The English have a commercial spirit, a love of money which has killed every sentiment of honor and every distinction of right and wrong.

English cowardice and sensuality are hidden behind unctuous, theological fine talk which is to us freethinking German heretics among all the sins of English nature the most repugnant.

— Reading No. 25 —

THE TRIPLE ALLIANCE, MAY 20, 1882*

Bismarck's system of secret alliance was designed to maintain German power as well as the peace of Europe. The central document of the system was the Triple Alliance.

✓   ✓   ✓

ARTICLE 1. The High Contracting Parties mutually promise peace and friendship and will enter into no alliance or engagement directed against any one of their States.

They engage to proceed to an exchange of ideas on political and economic questions of a general nature which may arise, and they further promise one another mutual support within the limits of their own interests.

ARTICLE 2. In case Italy, without direct provocation on her part, should be attacked by France for any reason whatsoever, the two other Contracting Parties shall be bound to lend help and assistance with all their forces to the Party attacked.

This same obligation shall devolve upon Italy in case of any aggression without direct provocation by France against Germany.

ARTICLE 3. If one, or two, of the High Contracting Parties, without direct provocation on their part, should chance to be attacked and to be engaged in a war with two or more Great Powers nonsignatory to the present Treaty, the *casus foederis* shall arise simultaneously for all the High Contracting Parties.

* Reprinted by permission of the publishers from Alfred F. Pribram, editor, *The Secret Treaties of Austria-Hungary, 1879-1914*. Translated by Archibald Gary Coolidge (Cambridge, Mass.: Harvard University Press, 1920) I, 65, 67, 69.

ARTICLE 4. In case a Great Power nonsignatory to the present Treaty should threaten the security of the states of one of the High Contracting Parties, and the threatened Party should find itself forced on that account to make war against it, the two others bind themselves to observe towards their Ally a benevolent neutrality. Each of them reserves to itself, in this case, the right to take part in the war, if it should see fit, to make common cause with its Ally. . . .

ARTICLE 6. The High Contracting Parties mutually promise secrecy as to the contents and existence of the present Treaty.

ARTICLE 7. The present Treaty shall remain in force during the space of five years, dating from the day of the exchange of ratifications.

ARTICLE 8. The ratifications of the present Treaty shall be exchanged at Vienna within three weeks, or sooner if may be.

In witness whereof the respective Plenipotentiaries have signed the present Treaty and have affixed thereto the seal of their arms.

Done at Vienna, the twentieth day of the month of May of the year one thousand eight hundred and eighty-two.

> (*L.S.*) KÁLNOKY
> (*L.S.*) H. VII OF REUSS
> (*L.S.*) C. ROBILANT

Ministerial Declaration

The Royal Italian Government declares that the provisions of the secret treaty concluded May 20, 1882, between Italy, Austria-Hungary, and Germany, cannot, as has been previously agreed, in any case be regarded as being directed against England.

— Reading No. 26 —

THE "URIAH LETTER," JUNE 9, 1892*

The bitterness between William II and Bismarck continued after the Chancellor's fall. In June, 1892, when Bismarck desired to go to Vienna to attend the wedding of his son Herbert to an Austrian princess, an official dispatch was addressed to the German Ambassador in Vienna. This so-called "Uriah Letter" stigmatized Bismarck as persona non grata.

✔   ✔   ✔

REICHSCHANCELLOR CAPRIVI TO THE AMBASSADOR IN VIENNA, PRINCE REUSS
June 9 (TO PRINCE REUSS, VIENNA. IMMEDIATE.)

After an audience with His Majesty, I inform Your Excellency of the following concerning the forthcoming marriage of Count Herbert Bismarck. The rumors of a reconciliation of Prince Bismarck and His Majesty do not take into account the indispensable presumption of a first step upon the part of the Prince. But even if this did take place, the reconciliation could never go so far that public opinion would take it that the Prince had won any kind of influence in the leadership of national affairs. His Majesty requests Your Excellency that, should the Prince or his family make any approach to Your Excellency's house, you limit yourself to the conventional forms, and avoid accepting any invitation to the wedding. His Majesty will not accept any notice of the wedding. You are instructed to inform Count Kálnoky of this fact in whatever manner may seem best to you. These indications as to behavior apply to the staff of the embassy as to yourself.

* *Reichsanzeiger,* July 7, 1892.

— Reading No. 27 —

THE KRUGER TELEGRAM, JANUARY 3, 1896*

The Jameson filibustering expedition in 1895 in the Transvaal Republic deepened the antagonism between Germany and Great Britain. Upon the collapse of the raid, William II sent a telegram of congratulations to President Kruger which was applauded in Germany but which embittered the English. The historian Gooch described the telegram as "the most disastrous error of the early years of the reign of William II."

*   *   *

I express to you my sincere congratulations that, supported by your people and without appealing for help to friendly Powers, you have succeeded by your energetic action against armed bands that invaded your country as disturbers of the peace, and have therefore been able to restore peace and safeguard the independence of the country from outside attacks.

— Reading No. 28 —

THE DAILY TELEGRAPH INTERVIEW, OCTOBER 28, 1908†

* *Die grosse Politik der europäischen Kabinette, 1871-1914* (40 vols.; Berlin, 1922-1926) XI, 31.
† *London Daily Telegraph*, October 28, 1908.

On October 28, 1908, The Daily Telegraph of London published an account of an interview between Kaiser William II and an unnamed British subject—one of the most significant interviews of the century. While appearing to present himself as a lover of peace, the Kaiser, through his own words, showed himself to be an advocate of the iron-fist policy in international relations. His faux pas was an incredible mistake that raised a storm of protest in both England and Germany and nearly led to the Kaiser's abdication. Historically, the Daily Telegraph interview marked a culminating point in Anglo-German political, economic, and naval rivalry that was to contribute to the outbreak of the catastrophe of 1914.

✓   ✓   ✓

We have received the following communication from a source of such unimpeachable authority that we can without hesitation comment on the obvious message which it conveys to the attention of the public.

Discretion is the first and last quality requisite in a diplomatist, and should still be observed by those who, like myself, have long passed from public into private life. Yet moments sometimes occur in the history of nations when a calculated indiscretion proves of the highest public service, and it is for that reason that I have decided to make known the substance of a lengthy conversation which it is my privilege to have had with His Majesty the German Emperor. I do so in the hope that it may help to remove that obstinate misconception of the character of the Kaiser's feelings toward England which, I fear, is deeply rooted in the Englishman's breast. It is the Emperor's sincere wish that it should be eradicated. He has given repeated proofs of his desire by word and deed. But, to speak frankly, his patience is sorely tried, now that he finds himself so continually misrepresented, and has so often experienced the mortification of finding that any momentary improvement of relations is followed by renewed outbursts of prejudice and a prompt return to the old attitude of suspicion.

As I have said, His Majesty honored me with a long conversation, and spoke with impulsive and unusual frankness.

"You English," he said, "are mad, mad, mad as March

hares. What has come over you that you are so completely given over to suspicions quite unworthy of a great nation? What more can I do than I have done? I declared with all the emphasis at my command, in my speech at Guildhall, that my heart is set upon peace, and that it is one of my dearest wishes to live on the best of terms with England. Have I ever been false to my word? Falsehood and prevarication are alien to my nature. My actions ought to speak for themselves, but you listen not to them but to those who misinterpret and distort them. That is a personal insult which I feel and resent. To be forever misjudged, to have my repeated offers of friendship weighed and scrutinized with jealous, mistrustful eyes, taxes my patience severely. I have said time after time that I am a friend of England, and your press—or, at least, a considerable section of it—bids the people of England refuse my proferred hand and insinuates that the other holds a dagger. How can I convince a nation against its will?

"I repeat," continued His Majesty, "that I am a friend of England, but you make things difficult for me. My task is not of the easiest. The prevailing sentiment among large sections of the middle and lower classes of my own people is not friendly to England. I am, therefore, so to speak, in a minority in my own land, but it is a minority of the best elements as it is in England with respect to Germany. That is another reason why I resent your refusal to accept my pledged word that I am the friend of England. I strive without ceasing to improve relations, and you retort that I am your archenemy. You make it hard for me. Why is it?"

Thereupon I ventured to remind His Majesty that not England alone, but the whole of Europe had viewed with disapproval the recent action of Germany in allowing the German consul to return from Tangier to Fez, and in anticipating the joint action of France and Spain by suggesting to the Powers that the time had come to Europe to recognize Mulai Hafiz as the new Sultan of Morocco.

His Majesty made a gesture of impatience.

"Yes," he said, "that is an excellent example of the way in which German action is misrepresented. First, then, as regards to the journey of Dr. Vassel. The German government, in sending Dr. Vassel back to his post at Fez, was only guided by the wish that he should look after the private interests of German subjects in that city, who cried for help and protection after the long absence of a consular representative." . . .

I suggested to His Majesty that an important and influential section of the German press had placed a very different interpretation upon the action of the German government, and, in fact, had given it their effusive approbation because they saw in it a strong act instead of mere words, and a decisive indication that Germany was once more about to intervene in the shaping of events in Morocco.

"There are mischief-makers," replied the Emperor, "in both countries. I will not attempt to weigh their relative capacity for misrepresentation. But the facts are as I have stated. There has been nothing in Germany's recent action with regard to Morocco which runs contrary to the explicit declaration of my love for peace which I made both at Guildhall and in my latest speech at Strasbourg."

His Majesty then reverted to the subject uppermost in his mind—his proved friendship for England. "I have referred," he said, "to the speeches in which I have done all that a sovereign can do to proclaim my good will. But, as actions speak louder than words, let me also refer to my acts. It is commonly believed in England that throughout the South African War Germany was hostile to her. German opinion undoubtedly was hostile—bitterly hostile. But what of official Germany? Let my critics ask themselves what brought to a sudden stop, and, indeed, to absolute collapse, the European tour of the Boer delegates, who were striving to obtain European intervention? They were feted in Holland, France gave them a rapturous welcome. They wished to come to Berlin, where the German people would have crowned them with flowers. But when they asked me to receive them—I refused. The agitation immediately died away, and the delegation returned empty-handed. Was that, I ask, the action of a secret enemy? . . ."

Such was the purport of the Emperor's conversation. He spoke with all the earnestness which marks his manner when speaking on deeply pondered subjects. I would ask my fellow countrymen who value the cause of peace to weigh what I have written, and to revise, if necessary, their estimate of the Kaiser and his friendship for England by His Majesty's own words. If they had enjoyed the privilege, which was mine, of hearing them spoken, they would doubt no longer either His Majesty's firm desire to live on the best of terms with England or his growing impatience at the persistent mistrust with which his offer of friendship is too often received.

— Reading No. 29 —

THE ZABERN AFFAIR, 1913*

The deep antagonism between Prussian militarism and German liberalism was brought to public attention in the spring of 1913 by an incident in the little town of Zabern in Alsace. A young German lieutenant struck a local shoemaker with his sword when the latter refused to make way for him on the street. Several clashes then took place between the local citizens and the military. The Zabern affair was a tempest in a teapot, but it was taken seriously in Germany. The reputation of the Prussian military emerged from the incident somewhat tarnished. Following are extracts from Chancellor von Bethmann-Hollweg's one-sided report to the Reichstag on December 3, 1913. The Chancellor made no mention of the arrogant and arbitrary behavior of the young lieutenant.

✓   ✓   ✓

GENTLEMEN: According to the results of the official inquiry, the events in Zabern took place as follows. First I should like to say that when I finish my talk the Minister of War will speak to you.

During a training hour, Lieutenant von Forstner was instructing a recruit on how he should handle himself

* *Stenographische Berichte über die Verhandlungen des Reichstages, 1913-1914,* Vol. 291, 6155-58.

in the event that he was attacked. In view of the many and sad occurrences of recent years, the Lieutenant was in the right to make this the subject of his instruction. On this occasion he said that in a certain eventuality there would be a money premium, which was made higher by a noncommissioned officer present. Putting up a money premium was, of course, improper. During his instruction, the Lieutenant called the man who was supposed to attack the recruit a "screwball" [*Wackes*]. At the same time the Lieutenant warned him about enlisting in the Foreign Legion. That was his good right. However, he did use a thoroughly improper expression when he spoke about service in the Foreign Legion. . . . In his instruction hour the Lieutenant on three occasions referred to Alsatians as "screwballs." . . .

Neither I nor the Minister of War want to excuse anything or keep anything secret. But what was behind these early events? Improper behavior of a young officer in the military barracks. Unpleasant but certainly not of world-shaking import. . . . The Alsatian people felt themselves to be insulted by use of the term "screwball." It has been said that there was a willful public affront to the people. That is not true, considering the circumstances as I have related them.

The use of the word "screwball" is now forbidden in military areas, and in agreement with the Minister of War, I can now say that the word will not be used again by our troops to describe the Alsatians.

The Alsatian deputies have been very sensitive about my use of the term "screwball." But I believe I am not imposing too much upon the gentlemen when I suggest that the Alsatians should not be more sensitive than other branches of our people. . . .

Gentlemen: Even though these events have been so unhappy, I believe that we should not cling to the past, but instead look to the future. Above all it is essential that the situation at Zabern, where the excitement originally arose, be brought back to normal. We must see to it that incidents of this kind do not recur. . . .

— Reading No. 30 —

GERMAN MILITARISM, 1914 AND 1939*

Confidence in military means as a solution for political ills has existed among all peoples. Jingoistic writing in Germany can be matched in varying degrees by examples from the writings of Déroulède and Barrès in France; Kipling and Maxse in England; D'Annunzio in Italy; and Hearst in the United States. It is true, nevertheless, that a comparatively large section of German intellectual life was imbued with militaristic ideas. This should not be attributed to any inborn or biological quality, but to the environmentalism of a peculiar socio-political and intellectual system geared to Prussianism with its accent on State-worship and discipline-duty-obedience. Below are excerpts from the pre-1914 writings of Friedrich von Bernhardi (1849-1930) and the pre-1939 work of Ewald Banse, Nazi Professor of Military Science at Brunswick Technical College.

✓   ✓   ✓

I

Bernhardi on War

War is a biological necessity of the first importance, a regulative element in the life of mankind which can-

---

* Friedrich von Bernhardi, *Deutschland und der nächste Krieg* (Stuttgart, 1911) translated by A. H. Powles (New York, 1914) pp. 18, 47, 288, 27; Ewald Banse, *Raum und Volk im Weltkriege,* translated by Alan Harris as *Germany Prepares for War* (London and New York, 1934) pp. 56-57.

not be dispensed with, since without it an unhealthy development will follow, which excludes every advancement of the race, and therefore all real civilization.

Under certain circumstances, it is not only the right but the moral and political duty of the statesman to bring about a war.

We must rouse in our people the unanimous wish for power in this sense together with the determination to sacrifice on the altar of patriotism, not only life and property, but also private views and preferences in the interests of the common welfare. Then alone shall we discharge our great duties of the future, grow into a World Power, and stamp a great part of humanity with the impress of the German Spirit.

Any action in favor of collective humanity outside the limits of the State and nationality is impossible. Such conceptions belong to the wide domain of Utopias.

II

Banse on Warlike Man versus Pacifist

The actively warlike man is the man who does not fight to live, but lives to fight. War is his element. His eagle eye is ever on the alert for chances and opportunities of fighting; with his slight frame, which looks as if it were built for cutting through obstacles, he comes down like a wolf on the fold. This born warrior hurls himself without thinking into the mêlée; so far from trying to avoid or mitigate a quarrel, he looks for it and greets it with a cheer. For him battle is the everlasting yea, the fulfillment and justification of existence. . . .

How utterly different . . . is the peace-loving man, the pacifist! Peace is the only state for which he is fitted and he will do anything to preserve it; he will endure any humiliation, including loss of liberty and even the most severe damage to his pocket, in order to avoid war. To this bourgeois or philistine, the warrior is the sworn foe, the deadly enemy who only exists to destroy his miserable rest. It remains a source of mixed wonder and horror to him that anybody can jeopardize his peace and security from mere pugnacity or on idealistic grounds. That is just the essential difference: the warrior . . . wagers his whole habitual existence, all he possesses, on the point of his sword, when it is a matter of maintaining his ego, his point of view, in a word, his honor, which is more to him than his individual life; the man of peace, be his muscles weak or strong, values honor and renown less than his own little life, which seems so great and important to him; he sets the individual destiny above the destiny of the nation.

— Reading No. 31 —

THE "WILLY-NICKY" TELEGRAMS, JULY 29-30, 1914*

Although he declined to renew the Reinsurance Treaty in 1890, William II did all in his power to maintain friendly personal relations with Nicholas II. "Willy" and "Nicky" maintained an affectionate correspondence in English for more than two decades preceding 1914. Both monarchs somewhat naïvely believed that their personal communications would do much to cement the good relations between Germany and Russia at a time when diplomatic relations between the two countries were steadily deteriorating.

✓   ✓   ✓

I

Kaiser to Tsar, July 29, 1:45 A.M.

It is with the gravest concern that I hear of the impression which the action of Austria against Servia is creating

* *Kautsky Documents, Die deutschen Dokumente zum Kriegsausbruch,* edited by Karl Kautsky, Graf Max Montgelas, and Prof. Walter Schücking (4 vols., Berlin, 1919) translated by the Carnegie Endowment for International Peace. Reprinted by permission of the Carnegie Endowment for International Peace. Nos. 335, 332, 359, 390.

in your country. The unscrupulous agitation that has been going on in Servia for years has resulted in the outrageous crime, to which Archduke Francis Ferdinand fell a victim. The spirit that led Servians to murder their own king and his wife still dominates the country. You will doubtless agree with me that we both, you and me, have a common interest as well as all Sovereigns to insist that all the persons morally responsible for the dastardly murder should receive their deserved punishment. In this case politics plays no part at all.

On the other hand, I fully understand how difficult it is for you and your Government to face the drift of your public opinion. Therefore, with regard to the hearty and tender friendship which binds us both from long ago with firm ties, I am exerting my utmost influence to induce the Austrians to deal straightly to arrive to a satisfactory understanding with you. I confidently hope that you will help me in my efforts to smooth over difficulties that may still arise.

Your very sincere and devoted friend and cousin

WILLY

II

Tsar to Kaiser, July 29, 8:20 P.M.

Am glad you are back. In this serious moment, I appeal to you to help me. An ignoble war has been declared to a weak country. The indignation in Russia shared fully by me is enormous. I foresee that very soon I shall be overwhelmed by the pressure forced upon me and be forced to take extreme measures which will lead to war. To try and avoid such a calamity as a European war I beg you in the name of our old friendship to do what you can to stop your allies from going too far.

III

Kaiser to Tsar, July 29, 6:30 P.M.

. . . I think a direct understanding between your Government and Vienna possible and desirable; and as I already telegraphed to you, my Government is continuing its exercises to promote it. Of course military measures on the part of Russia would be looked upon by Austria as a calamity we both wish to avoid and jeopardize my position as mediator which I readily accepted on your appeal to my friendship and my help.

IV

Tsar to Kaiser, July 30, 1:20 A.M.

Thank you heartily for your quick answer. Am sending Tatischev this evening with instructions. The military measures which have now come into force were decided five days ago for reasons of defence on account of Austria's preparations. I hope from all my heart that these measures won't in any way interfere with your part as mediator which I greatly value. We need your strong pressure on Austria to come to an understanding with us.

— Reading No. 32 —

WILLIAM II'S WAR SPEECHES, JULY-AUGUST, 1914*

The personality of William II was revealed in a series of bellicose and militarily pious speeches delivered upon the outbreak of World War I. Following are three characteristic examples.

✓   ✓   ✓

Speech from the Balcony of the Royal Palace, Berlin, July 31, 1914

A momentous hour has struck for Germany. Envious rivals everywhere force us to legitimate defense. The

* *Norddeutsche Allgemeine Zeitung*, August 2, 1914, p. 1; *Frankfurter Zeitung*, August 2, 1914, II, 1; *Neue Preussische Zeitung*, August 19, 1914, II, 1.

sword has been forced into our hands. I hope that in the event that my efforts to the very last moment do not succeed in bringing our opponents to reason and in preserving peace, we may use the sword, with the help of God, so that we may sheathe it again with honor. War will demand enormous sacrifices by the German people, but we shall show the enemy what it means to attack Germany. And so I commend you to God. Go forth into the churches, kneel down before God, and implore his help for our brave army.

Speech From the Balcony of the Royal Palace, Berlin, August 1, 1914

I thank you from the bottom of my heart for the expression of your loyalty and your esteem. When it comes to war, all parties cease and we are all brothers. One or another party has attacked me in peace time, but now I forgive them wholeheartedly. If our neighbors do not give us peace, then we hope and wish that our good German sword will come victorious out of this war!

Speech of William II to the Guards at Potsdam, August 18, 1914

Former generations as well as those who stand here today have often seen the soldiers of the First Guard Regiment and My Guards at this place. We were brought together then by an oath of allegiance which we swore before God. Today all have gathered to pray for the triumph of our weapons, for now that oath must be proved to the last drop of blood. The sword, which I have left in its scabbard for decades, shall decide.

I expect My First Guard Regiment on Foot and My Guards to add a new page of fame to their glorious history. The celebration today finds us confident in God in the Highest and remembering the glorious days of Leuthen, Chlum, and St. Privat. Our ancient fame is an appeal to the German people and their sword. And the entire German nation to the last man has grasped the sword. And so I draw the sword which with the help of God I have kept in its scabbard for decades. [*At this point the Kaiser drew his sword from its scabbard and held it high above his head.*]

The sword is drawn, and I cannot sheathe it again

without victory and honor. All of you shall and will see
to it that only in honor is it returned to the scabbard.
You are my guaranty that I can dictate peace to my
enemies. Up and at the enemy! Down with the enemies of
Brandenburg! Three cheers for our army!

— Reading No. 33 —

ORIGIN OF THE TERM, "A SCRAP OF PAPER," AUGUST 4, 1914*

*After German troops crossed the Belgian border on
the morning of August 4, 1914, Sir E. Goschen, the
British Ambassador in Berlin, called on Chancellor von
Bethmann-Hollweg for a final interview. Goschen's report to Sir Edward Grey reveals the origin of the famous
phrase, "a scrap of paper," which had an important effect
on world public opinion.*

✓   ✓   ✓

I found the Chancellor very agitated. His Excellency
at once began a harangue, which lasted for about twenty
minutes. He said that the step taken by His Majesty's
Government was terrible to a degree; just for a word—
"neutrality," a word which in war time had so often been
disregarded—just for a scrap of paper Great Britain was
going to make war on a kindred nation who desired
nothing better than to be friends with her. All his efforts
in that direction had been rendered useless by this last
terrible step, and the policy to which, as I knew, he had
devoted himself since his accession to office had tumbled
down like a house of cards. What we had done was un-

---

* *Collected Diplomatic Documents Relating to the Outbreak
of the European War* (London, 1915) "British Diplomatic
Correspondence," No. 160, p. 111.

thinkable; it was like striking a man from behind while he was fighting for his life against two assailants. He held Great Britain responsible for all the terrible events that might happen.

— Reading No. 34 —

THE *HASSLIED*, 1914*

Ernst Lissauer's Hasslied, "Hymn of Hate Against England," *written in 1914, was effectively used by Allied propagandists in World War I. Following are the first two stanzas.*

French and Russian they matter not,
A blow for a blow and a shot for a shot;
We love them not, we hate them not,
We hold the Weichsel and Vosges-gate,
We have but one and only hate,
We love as one, we hate as one,
We have one foe and one alone.

He is known to you all, he is known to you all
He crouches behind the dark grey flood,
Full of envy, of rage, of craft, of gall,
Cut off by waves that are thicker than blood.
Come, let us stand at the Judgment place,
An oath to swear to, face to face,
An oath of bronze no wind can shake,
An oath for our sons and their sons to take.
Come, hear the word, repeat the word,
Throughout the Fatherland make it heard.

* Originally published in *Jugend* (1914). Translated by Barbara Henderson in *The New York Times*.

We will never forego our hate,
We have but one single hate,
We love as one, we hate as one,
We have one foe, and one alone—
ENGLAND!

— Reading No. 35 —

MANIFESTO OF THE NINETY-THREE GERMAN INTELLECTUALS, 1914*

Upon the outbreak of World War I, German university professors and men of science addressed a letter to the world defending Germany's course. A selection of the signatures given below indicates the stature of the scholars who signed the document.

✔   ✔   ✔

TO THE CIVILIZED WORLD!

As representatives of German Science and Art, we hereby protest to the civilized world against the lies and calumnies with which our enemies are endeavoring to stain the honor of Germany in her hard struggle for existence—in a struggle that has been forced on her.

The iron mouth of events has proved the untruth of the fictitious German defeats; consequently misrepresentation and calumny are all the more eagerly at work. As heralds of truth we raise our voices against these.

* A. Morel-Fatio, *Les Versions allemande et française du manifeste dit des intellectuels allemands dit des quatre-vingt-treize,* as quoted in R. H. Lutz, *Fall of the German Empire* (Stanford University, California, 1932) I, 74-78.

It is not true that Germany is guilty of having caused this war. Neither the people, the Government, nor the "Kaiser" wanted war. . . .

It is not true that we trespassed in neutral Belgium. It has been proved that France and England had resolved on such a trespass, and it has likewise been proved that Belgium had agreed to their doing so. It would have been suicide on our part not to have been beforehand.

It is not true that the life and property of a single Belgian citizen was injured by our soldiers without the bitterest defense having made it necessary. . . .

It is not true that our troops treated Louvain brutally. Furious inhabitants having treacherously fallen upon them in their quarters, our troops with aching hearts were obliged to fire a part of the town, as punishment. The greatest part of Louvain has been preserved. . . .

It is not true that our warfare pays no respects to international laws. It knows no undisciplined cruelty. But in the east, the earth is saturated with the blood of women and children unmercifully butchered by the wild Russian troops, and in the west, dumdum bullets mutilate the breasts of our soldiers. . . .

It is not true that the combat against our so-called militarism is not a combat against our civilization, as our enemies hypocritically pretend it is. Were it not for German militarism, German civilization would long since have been extirpated. . . .

We cannot wrest the poisonous weapon—the lie— out of the hands of our enemies. All we can do is proclaim to all the world, that our enemies are giving false witness against us. . . .

Have faith in us! Believe, that we shall carry on this war to the end as a civilized nation, to whom the legacy of a Goethe, a Beethoven, and a Kant, is just as sacred as its own hearths and homes.

> EMIL VON BEHRING, Professor of Medicine, Marburg
> Prof. PAUL EHRLICH, Frankfort on the Main
> FRITZ HABER, Professor of Chemistry, Berlin
> ERNST HAECKEL, Professor of Zoology, Jena
> Prof. ADOLF VON HARNACK, General Director of the Royal Library, Berlin

KARL LAMPRECHT, Professor of History, Leipzig
MAX LIEBERMAN, Berlin
MAX PLANCK, Professor of Physics, Berlin
Prof. MAX REINHARDT, Director of the German
　Theatre, Berlin
WILHELM RÖNTGEN, Professor of Physics, Munich
GUSTAV VON SCHMOLLER, Professor of National
　Economy, Berlin. . . .

— Reading No. 36 —

THE ZIMMERMANN NOTE, JANUARY 19, 1917 *

On January 19, 1917, the German Foreign Secretary, Alfred Zimmermann, sent a note to the German Ambassador in Mexico proposing to Mexico an alliance providing for a joint war against the United States. Interception and publication of the note in the United States greatly strengthened the demand for war, especially in the hitherto lukewarm Southwest, which Germany proposed to cede to Mexico.

✓　　　　✓　　　　✓

Berlin, January 19, 1917

On the first of February we intend to begin submarine warfare unrestricted. In spite of this, it is our intention to endeavor to keep neutral the United States of America.

If this attempt is not successful, we propose an alliance on the following basis with Mexico: That we shall make war together and together make peace. We shall give general financial support, and it is understood that Mexico is to reconquer the lost territory in New Mexico, Texas,

* *Congressional Record*, LVI (March 1, 1917) Part 1, pp. 680-81.

and Arizona. The details are left to you for settlement.

You are instructed to inform the President of Mexico of the above in the greatest confidence as soon as it is certain that there will be an outbreak of war with the United States and suggest that the President of Mexico, on his own initiative, should communicate with Japan suggesting adherence at once to this plan; at the same time, offer to mediate between Germany and Japan.

Please call to the attention of the President of Mexico that the employment of ruthless submarine warfare now promises to compel England to make peace in a few months.

ZIMMERMANN

— Reading No. 37 —

THE TREATY OF BREST LITOVSK, MARCH 3, 1918*

After the November Revolution of 1917, which brought the Bolsheviks to power, the Russians signed the Treaty of Brest Litovsk, by which they ceded to Germany nearly all the territory they had acquired in Europe since the time of Peter the Great. The harsh treaty indicated to the Allies what was in store for them if they were to lose the war.

✓ ✓ ✓

ARTICLE 1. Germany, Austria-Hungary, Bulgaria, and Turkey on the one part and Russia on the other declare that the state of war between them has ended. They are resolved henceforth to live in peace and friendship with one another.

ARTICLE 2. The contracting parties will refrain from any agitation or propaganda against the Government or

* *Reichsgesetzblatt*, No. 77, June 11, 1918, pp. 479-90, *passim.*

public and military institutions of the other party. In so far as this obligation falls on Russia, it also holds good for the territories occupied by the Powers of the Quadruple Alliance.

ARTICLE 3. The territories lying to the west of the line agreed upon by the contracting parties which formerly belonged to Russia will no longer be under Russian sovereignty. . . . The exact line will be established by a Russo-German commission.

ARTICLE 4. As soon as the general peace is concluded and Russian demobilization is completely carried out, Germany will evacuate the territory lying to the east of the line designated in paragraph 1 of Article 3. . . .

ARTICLE 5. Russia will without delay fully demobilize her army. . . .

Furthermore, Russia will either bring her warships into Russian ports . . . or disarm them forthwith. . . .

The barred zone of the Arctic Ocean continues as such until the conclusion of a general peace. . . .

ARTICLE 8. Prisoners of war of both parties shall be released to return to their homeland. . . .

— Reading No. 38 —

EXTRACTS FROM THE TREATY OF VERSAILLES, JUNE 28, 1919*

The Treaty of Versailles, between the Allies and Germany, was signed in the Hall of Mirrors in the palace of Versailles on June 28, 1919. Both the time and the place were selected to humiliate Germany—the time was the fifth anniversary of the assassination at Sarajevo, and

* United States, 66th Congress, 1st Session, Senate Document No. 49, *Treaty of Peace with Germany* (Washington, 1919).

the place was the same hall where, in 1871, the German Empire had been proclaimed. The treaty was ratified by the signatories in Paris on January 10, 1920. Following are the more important articles.

✓   ✓   ✓

PART II

Boundaries of Germany [omitted]

PART III

Political Clauses for Europe

ARTICLE 31. Germany, recognizing that the Treaties of April 19, 1839, which established the status of Belgium before the war, no longer conform to the requirements of the situation, consents to the abrogation of the said treaties and undertakes immediately to recognize and to observe whatever conventions may be entered into by the Principal Allied and Associated Powers, or by any of them, in concert with the Governments of Belgium and of the Netherlands, to replace the said Treaties of 1839. If her formal adhesion should be required to such conventions or to any of their stipulations, Germany undertakes immediately to give it. . . .

ARTICLE 42. Germany is forbidden to maintain or construct any fortifications either on the left bank of the Rhine or on the right bank to the west of a line drawn 50 kilometres to the East of the Rhine. . . .

ARTICLE 45. As compensation for the destruction of the coal-mines in the north of France and as part payment towards the total reparation due from Germany for the damage resulting from the war, Germany cedes to France in full and absolute possession, with exclusive rights of exploitation, unencumbered and free from all debts and charges of any kind, the coal-mines situated in the Saar Basin as defined in Article 48. . . .

ARTICLE 51. The territories which were ceded to Germany in accordance with the Preliminaries of Peace signed at Versailles on February 26, 1871, and the Treaty of Frankfurt of May 10, 1871, are restored to French sovereignty as from the date of the Armistice of November 11, 1918.

The provisions of the Treaties establishing the delimitation of the frontiers before 1871 shall be restored. . . .

ARTICLE 80. Germany acknowledges and will respect strictly the independence of Austria. . . .

ARTICLE 81. Germany, in conformity with the action already taken by the Allied and Associated Powers, recognizes the complete independence of the Czecho-Slovak State. . . .

ARTICLE 87. Germany, in conformity with the action already taken by the Allied and Associated Powers, recognizes the complete independence of Poland, and renounces in her favour all rights and title over the territory [of Poland].

The boundaries of Poland not laid down in the present Treaty will be subsequently determined by the Principal Allied and Associated Powers. . . .

PART IV

German Rights and Interests Outside Germany

ARTICLE 119. Germany renounces in favour of the Principal Allied and Associated Powers all her rights and titles over her oversea possessions. . . .

PART V

Military, Naval, and Air Claims

ARTICLE 160. By a date which must not be later than March 31, 1920, the German Army must not comprise more than seven divisions of infantry and three divisions of cavalry.

After that date the total number of effectives in the Army of the States constituting Germany must not exceed one hundred thousand men, including officers and establishments of depots. The Army shall be devoted exclusively to the maintenance of order within the territory and to the control of the frontiers.

The total effective strength of officers, including the personnel of staffs, whatever their composition, must not exceed four thousand.

. . . The Great German General Staff and all similar organisations shall be dissolved and may not be reconstituted in any form.

ARTICLE 180. All fortified works, fortresses and field works situated in German territory to the west of a line drawn fifty kilometres to the east of the Rhine shall be disarmed and dismantled.

ARTICLE 181. After the expiration of a period of two months from the coming into force of the present Treaty the German naval forces in commission must not exceed:

6 battleships of the *Deutschland* or *Lothringen* type,
6 light cruisers,
12 destroyers,
12 torpedo boats,

or an equal number of ships constructed to replace them as provided in Article 190.

No submarines are to be included.

All other warships, except where there is provision to the contrary in the present Treaty, must be placed in reserve or devoted to commercial purposes. . . .

ARTICLE 198. The armed forces of Germany must not include any military or naval air forces. . . .

PART VI

Reparation

ARTICLE 231. The Allied and Associated Governments affirm and Germany accepts the responsibility of Germany and her allies for causing all the loss and damage to which the Allied and Associated Governments and their nationals have been subjected as a consequence of the war imposed upon them by the aggression of Germany and her allies. . . .

PART X

Special Provisions

ARTICLE 245. Within six months after the coming into force of the present Treaty the German Government must restore to the French Government the trophies, archives, historical souvenirs or works of art carried away from France by the German authorities in the course of the war of 1870-1871 and during this last war. . . .

ARTICLE 246. Within six months from the coming into force of the present Treaty, Germany will restore to

His Majesty the King of the Hedjaz the original Koran of the Caliph Othman, which was removed from Medina by the Turkish authorities and is stated to have been presented to the ex-Emperor William II.

Within the same period Germany will hand over to His Britannic Majesty's Government the skull of the Sultan Mkwawa which was removed from the Protectorate of German East Africa and taken to Germany. . . .

PART XIV

Guarantees

ARTICLE 428. As a guarantee for the execution of the present Treaty by Germany, the German territory situated to the west of the Rhine, together with the bridgeheads, will be occupied by Allied and Associated troops for a period of fifteen years from the coming into force of the present Treaty. . . .

ARTICLE 431. If before the expiration of the period of fifteen years Germany complies with all the undertakings resulting from the present Treaty, the occupying forces will be withdrawn immediately.

— Reading No. 39 —

THE WEIMAR CONSTITUTION OF THE GERMAN REICH, AUGUST 11, 1919*

The first draft of the Weimar Constitution was prepared by a Dr. Hugo Preuss, a political-science teacher, and this was, in the main, adopted. Passed on July 31, 1919,

* *Die Verfassung des Deutschen Reiches von 11. August, 1919* (Reclams Universal Bibliothek, No. 6051, Leipzig, 1930).

at its third reading, it was signed by Ebert and the Reich Cabinet on August 11 and published three days later. The National Assembly then elected Ebert president of the Reich—without the formality of a popular vote.

The German people, united in its ethnic elements and impelled by the will to renew and strengthen its Reich in liberty and justice, to serve the ends of peace on the domestic scene and abroad, and to further social progress, has established this constitution.

PART 1: STRUCTURE AND FUNCTION OF THE REICH

Chapter 1: Reich and Lands

ARTICLE 1. The German Reich is a Republic. The power of the State is derived from the people.

ARTICLE 2. The territory of the Reich consists of the territories of the German Lands. Other territories may be taken into the Reich through legislation of the Reich, if their people desire it through the right of self-determination.

ARTICLE 3. The colors of the Reich are black, red, and gold. The flag of the merchant fleet is black, white, and red, with the colors of the Reich in the upper inside corner.

ARTICLE 4. The generally accepted rules of international law are to be considered as binding integral parts of the law of the German Reich.

ARTICLE 5. The powers of the State in matters concerning the Reich shall be exercised through the organs of the Reich on the basis of the Reich's Constitution, in matters concerning the Lands (member states) through the organs of the Lands on the basis of the constitutions of the Lands. . . .

ARTICLE 14. The laws of the Reich shall be carried out by the authorities of the Lands, in so far as the laws of the Reich do not specify otherwise. . . .

Chapter 2: The Reichstag

ARTICLE 20. The *Reichstag* is composed of the delegates of the German people.

ARTICLE 21. The delegates represent the entire people. They are subject only to their own conscience and are not bound by any instructions.

ARTICLE 22. The delegates are elected by universal, equal, direct, and secret ballot by men and women over twenty years of age, according to the principles of proportional representation. The voting day must fall on a Sunday or a public holiday.

ARTICLE 23. The delegates to the Reichstag shall be elected for four years. The new election must take place at the latest on the sixtieth day after its expiration. The Reichstag shall meet for the first time at the latest on the thirtieth day after its election. . . .

ARTICLE 25. The President of the Reich may dissolve the Reichstag, but only one time for the same reason. The new election must take place at the latest on the sixtieth day after its dissolution. . . .

Chapter 3: The Reich President and the Reich Cabinet

ARTICLE 41. The Reich President shall be elected by the entire German people. Every German who has completed his thirty-fifth year is eligible to the office. . . .

ARTICLE 42. The Reich President shall take the following oath upon assuming his position: "I swear that I shall dedicate my power to the German people, to further its welfare, to prevent injury to it, to protect the Constitution and the laws of the Reich, conscientiously to fulfill my duties, and to exercise justice for every man." The addition of a religious oath is permissible.

ARTICLE 43. The tenure of the Reich President shall last seven years. . . .

ARTICLE 48. If a Land fails to fulfil the duties incumbent upon it according to the Constitution or the laws of the Reich, the Reich President can force it to do so with the help of the armed forces.

The Reich President may, if the public safety and order in the German Reich are considerably disturbed or endangered, take such measures as are necessary to restore public safety and order. If necessary he may intervene with the help of the armed forces. For this purpose he may temporarily suspend, either partially or wholly, the

Fundamental Rights established in Articles 114, 115, 117, 118, 123, 124 and 153.*

The Reich President shall inform the Reichstag without delay of all measures taken under Paragraph 1 or Paragraph 2 of this Article. On demand by the Reichstag the measures shall be repealed. . . .

ARTICLE 52. The Reich cabinet consists of the Reich Chancellor and the Reich ministers.

ARTICLE 53. The Reich Chancellor and on his recommendation the Reich ministers shall be named and dismissed by the Reich President.

ARTICLE 54. The Reich Chancellor and the Reich ministers shall enjoy the confidence of the Reichstag during their tenure of office. Each of them must resign when the Reichstag through explicit resolution withdraws its confidence. . . .

Chapter 4: The Reichsrat

ARTICLE 60. A *Reichsrat* shall be established to represent the German Lands in legislation and for the administration of the Reich.

ARTICLE 61. Each Land shall have at least one vote in the *Reichsrat*. For the larger Lands there shall be one vote for each 700,000 inhabitants. An excess of at least 350,000 inhabitants shall be counted as the full 700,000. No Land shall have more than two-fifths of all the votes. . . .

Chapter 5: The Reich Promulgation of Laws

ARTICLE 68. Projected laws shall come from the Reich cabinet or from the Reichstag. The laws of the Reich shall be promulgated by the Reichstag. . . .

PART 2: FUNDAMENTAL RIGHTS AND DUTIES OF THE GERMANS

* The other articles mentioned in Article 48: Article 114 (freedom of the individual); Article 115 (freedom of residence); Article 117 (secrecy of postal, telegraph, and telephone communications); Article 118 (freedom of expression); Article 123 (freedom of assembly); Article 124 (freedom of organization); and 153 (personal property guarantee).

Chapter 1: The Individual Person

ARTICLE 109. All Germans are equal before the law. In principle men and women possess the same civil rights and duties. Public legal privileges or disadvantages due to birth or rank are to be abolished. Titles of nobility shall be regarded only as part of the name, and shall no longer be bestowed. Titles shall be bestowed only to indicate an office or profession; academic degrees are not thereby affected. Orders and decorations shall not be conferred by the State. No German shall accept titles or orders from a foreign government.

ARTICLE 110. Citizenship in the Reich and in the Lands shall be acquired and lost according to the provisions of a Reich law. Every citizen of a Land is at the same time a citizen of the Reich. Every German has in every Land of the Reich the same rights and duties as the citizens of that Land.

ARTICLE 111. All Germans enjoy freedom of travel and residence throughout the whole Reich. Everyone has the right to live and settle in any place in the Reich, to acquire real estate, and to pursue any means of livelihood. Any restrictions shall require a Reich law.

ARTICLE 114. The freedom of the person is inviolable. Any curtailment or deprivation of personal freedom by a public authority shall take place only on a legal basis. Those persons who have been deprived of their freedom shall be informed, at the latest on the following day, concerning by whose authority and for what reasons they have been deprived of their freedom; they shall have the opportunity without delay of submitting objections to their loss of freedom.

ARTICLE 115. The dwelling of every German is his sanctuary and is inviolable. Any exceptions may be made only by law.

ARTICLE 116. An act can be punished only if the penalty has been stated by law previous to the commission of the act.

ARTICLE 117. The secrecy of letters and all postal, telegraphic, and telephone communications is inviolable. Exceptions can be made only by Reich legislation.

ARTICLE 118. Every German has the right, within the limits of the general law, to express his opinions freely in speech, in writing, in print, in picture form, or in any other way. From this right there shall be no condition or work or employment to detract him, and no person shall be placed in a position of disadvantage if he has made use of this right. Censorship is forbidden, but deviations may be made from this rule by law in the special case of moving pictures. Legal provisions may be made for counteracting pornography and obscene publications and for protecting youth at public plays and entertainments. . . .

Chapter 2: The General Welfare

ARTICLE 123. All Germans have the right to assemble peacefully and unarmed without giving previous notice and without any special permission. Previous notification for open-air assemblies may be required by a Reich law; such a law may prohibit these meetings when there is a present danger to the public welfare.

ARTICLE 124. All Germans possess the right to form associations or societies for any purpose not contrary to criminal law. This right shall not be curtailed by preventive measures. The same provisions apply to religious associations or societies. Every association has the right to become incorporated according to the provisions of the civil law. This right shall not be denied to any association on the ground that its aims are political, socio-political, or religious.

ARTICLE 125. The liberty and secrecy of the vote are guaranteed. . . .

ARTICLE 135. All inhabitants of the Reich enjoy full freedom of religion and conscience. . . .

Chapter 4: Education and the Schools

ARTICLE 142. Art and science and their teaching are free. . . .

ARTICLE 145. Attendance at school is obligatory. . . .

ARTICLE 148. Moral training, a sense of civic responsibility, personal and vocational efficiency, in a spirit of national German sentiment and international conciliation, shall be the aim in all schools. . . .

Chapter 5: Economic Life

ARTICLE 151. Economic life shall be made compatible with the principles of justice, the aim being the attainment of humane conditions of existence for all. . . .

ARTICLE 153. Personal property is guaranteed by the Constitution. Acquisition of property and its limitation shall be subject to legislation. . . . Property is guaranteed, but its use shall be subservient to the general welfare. . . .

ARTICLE 160. For the maintenance of health and the capacity to work, for the protection of maternity, and for protection against the economic consequences of age, illness, and the vicissitudes of life, the Reich shall organize a comprehensive system of insurance, in which the insured persons shall cooperate to a considerable extent. . . .

FINAL PROVISIONS

ARTICLE 181. The German people have passed and adopted this Constitution through their National Assembly. It comes into force with the date of its proclamation.

SCHWARZBURG, AUGUST 11, 1919

The Reich President

EBERT

The Reich Cabinet

BAUER

ERZBERGER   HERMAN MÜLLER   DR. DAVID

NOSKE   SCHMIDT

SCHLICKE   GIESBERTS   DR. BAYER

DR. BELL

— Reading No. 40 —

THE 25-POINT PROGRAM OF THE NATIONAL SOCIALIST GERMAN WORKERS' PARTY, FEBRUARY 25, 1920*

* *The Program of the National Socialist Workers' Party* (Munich, 1920).

The original program of the National Socialist German Workers' Party envisaged a "Third Reich" and a Greater Germany. Note how the program stressed anti-Semitism and anti-Bolshevism.

The program of the German Workers' Party is limited as to period. The leaders have no intention, once the aims announced in it have been achieved, of setting up fresh ones, merely in order to increase the discontent of the masses artificially and so ensure the continued existence of the party.

1. We demand the union of all Germans to form a Great Germany on the basis of the right of self-determination of nations.

2. We demand equality of rights for the German people in its dealings with other nations, and abolition of the Peace Treaties of Versailles and Saint-Germain.

3. We demand land and territory [colonies] for the nourishment of our people and for settling our surplus population.

4. None but members of the nation [*Volksgenossen*] may be citizens of the State. None but those of German blood, whatever their creed, may be members of the nation. No Jew, therefore, may be a member of the nation.

5. Any one who is not a citizen of the State may live in Germany only as a guest and must be subject to laws for aliens.

6. The right of voting for the leaders and laws of the State is to be enjoyed by the citizen of the State alone. . . .

7. We demand that the State shall make it its first duty to promote the industry and livelihood of citizens of the State. If it is not possible to nourish the entire population of the State, foreign nationals [non-citizens] must be excluded from the Reich.

8. All further non-German immigration must be prevented. We demand that all non-Germans who entered Germany subsequent to August 2nd, 1914, shall be compelled forthwith to depart from the Reich.

9. All citizens of the State shall be equal as regards rights and duties.

10. It must be the first duty of each citizen of the State to work with his mind or with his body. The activities of the individual may not clash with the interests of the whole, but must proceed within the frame of the community and be for the general good.

We demand therefore:

11. Abolition of all incomes unearned by work.

12. In view of the enormous sacrifice of life and property demanded of a nation by every war, personal enrichment due to a war must be regarded as a crime against the nation. We demand therefore ruthless confiscation of all war gains.

13. We demand nationalization of all businesses which have been up to the present formed into companies [trusts].

14. We demand that all the profits from wholesale trade shall be shared out.

15. We demand extensive development of provision for old age.

16. We demand creation and maintenance of a healthy middle class, immediate communalization of department stores, and their lease at a cheap rate to small traders, and extreme consideration for all small purveyors to the State, district authorities, and smaller localities.

17. We demand land reform suitable to our national requirements, passing of a law for confiscation without compensation of land for common purposes; abolition of interest on land loans, and prevention of all speculation in land.

18. We demand a ruthless struggle against those whose activities are injurious to the common interest. Common criminals against the nation, usurers, profiteers, etc., must be punished with death, whatever their creed or race.

19. We demand that the Roman Law, which serves the materialistic world order, shall be replaced by a German legal system.

20. With the aim of opening to every capable and industrious German the possibility of higher education and of thus obtaining advancement, the State must consider a thorough reconstruction of our national system of education. . . .

21. The State must see to raising the standard of health in the nation by protecting mothers and infants, prohibit-

ing child labor, increasing bodily efficiency by obligatory gymnastics and sports laid down by law, and by extensive support of clubs engaged in the bodily development of the young.

22. We demand abolition of a paid army, and formation of a national army.

23. We demand legal warfare against conscious political lying and its dissemination in the press. . . .

24. We demand liberty for all religious denominations in the State, so far as they are not a danger to, and do not militate against the moral feelings of, the German race. . . .

25. That all the foregoing may be realized, we demand the creation of a strong central power of the State. Unquestioned authority of the politically centralized Parliament over the entire Reich and its organizations; and formation of Chambers for classes and occupations for the purpose of carrying out the general laws promulgated by the Reich in the various states of the confederation.

The leaders of the party swear to go straight forward— if necessary to sacrifice their lives—in securing fulfilment of the foregoing points.

— Reading No. 41 —

THE PHILOSOPHY OF NATIONAL SOCIALISM*

"At every stage of my life," said Hitler, "I come back to Richard Wagner." The Nazi Fuehrer correctly evaluated the part played by his spiritual master in the development

* Richard Wagner: *Gesammelte Schriften,* translated by William Ashton Ellis (8 vols.; London, 1892-1899) *passim;* and Adolf Hitler, *Mein Kampf,* 805th to 809th ed. (Munich, 1943) *passim.*

*of Nazi extremism. The following précis shows the close
affinity between Wagnerian and Hitlerian views.*

✓   ✓   ✓

The State

WAGNER: In the State the unit must offer a part of his own egoism for the welfare of the majority.
—The intrinsic object of the State *is stability,* the maintenance of quiet.

HITLER: The State is only a means towards an end. Its highest aim is the care and maintenance of those primeval racial elements [*Urelemente*] which create the beauty and dignity of a higher civilization.

The Volk

WAGNER: The *Volk* consists of those who think instinctively.
—The *Volk* deals unconsciously and, for that very reason, from a Nature-instinct.

HITLER: The dead mechanism [of the old State] must be replaced by a living organism based on the herd instinct, which appears when all are of one blood.

The Leader

WAGNER: We must now seek the Hero of the future, who turns against the ruin of his race.
—Barbarossa-Siegfried will some day return to save the German people in time of deepest need.

HITLER: One must never forget it: the majority can never replace the leader. It [the majority] is not only stupid but cowardly. You cannot get one wise man out of a hundred fools, and a heroic decision cannot come out of a hundred cowards.

German Superiority

WAGNER: The true foundation of continued renovation has remained the German nature.
—In *something* EVERY German is akin to his great masters.
Genius and the German people have a certain something in common.

HITLER: It ought to be a greater honor to be a street-cleaner of the German Reich than king of a foreign power.

The Jews

WAGNER: The Jew is the plastic demon of the decline of mankind.

HITLER: The Jews are parasites on the bodies of other peoples; they make states within the State.

Anti-Rationalism

WAGNER: We must be brave enough to deny our intellect
—The *Volk* must burst the chain of hindering consciousness.

HITLER: The educational system of the Folkish-State finds its crowning work in burning into the brains and heart of the youth intrusted to it an instinctual and understanding sense of race and race feeling.

Democracy

WAGNER: Democracy is totally un-German, a translated thing from elsewhere.
—Franco-Judaico-German democracy is a disgusting thing.

HITLER: Democracy is a rule by crazy brains.
—The German Republic is a monstrosity of human mechanism.

France

WAGNER: Germany's mission lies in extricating the world from the materialistic civilization of the French.

HITLER: France is and remains the inexorable enemy of Germany.
—France has made so much progress in her Negroization [*in seiner Venegerung*] that one can in fact speak of the creation of an African state on European territory.

— Reading No. 42 —

NAZI RACIALISM*

Nazi racialism became almost completely irrational with this passage by Hermann Gauch, a specialist in Rassenkunde and Rassenforschung (the study of human breeds and races).

✓   ✓   ✓

Generally speaking, the Nordic race alone can emit sounds of untroubled clearness, whereas among non-Nordic men and races, the pronunciation is impurer, the individual sounds more confused and more like the noises made by animals, such as barking, snoring, sniffing, and squeaking. That birds can learn to talk better than other animals is explained by the fact that their mouths are Nordic in structure—that is to say, high, narrow, and short-tongued. The shape of the Nordic gum allows a superior movement of the tongue, which is the reason why Nordic talking and singing are fuller.

This passage may be compared with the following description of "Jewish sounds" by the composer, Richard Wagner, spiritual predecessor of National Socialism.

✓   ✓   ✓

The Jew speaks the language of the nation in whose midst he dwells from generation to generation, but he always speaks it as an alien. Our whole European art and civilization have remained to the Jew a foreign tongue. In this speech, this art, the Jew can only after-speak and after-patch—not truly make a poem of his words, an artwork of his doings. In the peculiarities of Semitic pronunciation the first thing that strikes our ear as quite

* Hermann Gauch, *Neue Grundlagen des Rassenforschung* (Berlin, n.d.) p. 165. Richard Wagner, *Gesammelte Schriften,* translated by William Ashton Ellis (8 vols.; London, 1892-1899) III, 84-85.

outlandish and unpleasant, in the Jew's production of the voice-sounds, is a creaking, squeaking, buzzing snuffle [*ein zischender, schrillender, summsender und murksender Lautausdruck*]. This mode of speaking acquires at once the character of an intolerably jumbled blabber [*eines unerträglich verwirrten Geplappers*]. The cold indifference of his peculiar blubber [*Gelabber*] never by chance rises to the ardor of a higher heartfelt passion.

— Reading No. 43 —

THE HORST WESSEL SONG, 1933*

The official Nazi anthem was written by a young street-fighter, Horst Wessel, who was made a national hero after his violent death.

✓   ✓   ✓

I

Hold high the banner! Close the hard ranks serried!
S.A. marches on with sturdy stride.
Comrades, by Red Front and Reaction killed, are buried,
But march with us in image at our side.

II

Gangway! Gangway now for the Brown Battalions!
For the Storm Trooper clear roads o'er the land!
The Swastika gives hope to our entranced millions,
The day for freedom and for bread's at hand.

III

The trumpet blows its shrill and final blast!
Prepared for war and battle here we stand.

* Translated by the editor.

Soon Hitler's banners will wave unchecked at last,
The end of German slav'ry in our land!

— Reading No. 44 —

THE NUREMBERG LAWS ON CITIZENSHIP AND RACE, SEPTEMBER-NOVEMBER, 1935 *

The most spectacular and immediate consequence of the Nazi triumph was the reign of anti-Semitism. From September to November, 1935, Hitler introduced the so-called Nuremberg, or Ghetto Laws, which placed anti-Semitism in the category of legal legislation. This was the first time in history that prejudice and intolerance were deliberately incorporated into the laws of a nation.

✓   ✓   ✓

I. The Reich Citizenship Law of September 15, 1935

The Reichstag has adopted by unanimous vote the following law which is herewith promulgated.

ARTICLE 1. (1) A subject of the State is one who belongs to the protective union of the German Reich, and who, therefore, has specific obligations to the Reich.

(2) The status of subject is to be acquired in accordance with the provisions of the Reich and the State Law of Citizenship.

ARTICLE 2. (1) A citizen of the Reich may be only

* *Reichsgesetzblatt*, 1935, No. 100, September 15, 1935, I 1142-47.

that subject who is of German or kindred blood, and who, through his behavior, shows that he is both desirous and personally fit to serve loyally the German people and the Reich. . . .

ARTICLE 3. The Reich Minister of the Interior, in conjunction with the Deputy to the *Fuehrer* will issue the required legal and administrative decrees for the implementation and amplification of this law.

Promulgated: September 16, 1935.

In force: September 30, 1935.

1. a. First Supplementary Decree of November 14, 1935

On the basis of Article 3 of the Reich Law of Citizenship of September 15, 1935, the following is hereby decreed:

ARTICLE 1. (1) Until further provisions concerning citizenship papers, all subjects of German or kindred blood who possessed the right to vote in the Reichstag elections when the Law of Citizenship came into effect, shall, for the present, possess the rights of Reich citizens. The same shall be true of those upon whom the Reich Minister of the Interior, in conjunction with the Deputy to the *Fuehrer*, shall confer citizenship. . . .

ARTICLE 2. (1) The provisions of Article 1 shall apply also to subjects who are of mixed Jewish blood.

(2) An individual of mixed Jewish blood is one who is descended from one or two grandparents who, racially, were full Jews, in so far that he is not a Jew. . . . Full-blooded Jewish grandparents are those who belonged to the Jewish religious community.

ARTICLE 3. Only citizens of the Reich, as bearers of full political rights, can exercise the right of voting in political matters, and have the right to hold public office. The Reich Minister of the Interior, or any agency he empowers, can make exceptions during the transition period on the matter of holding public office. These measures do not apply to matters concerning religious organizations. . . .

ARTICLE 7. The *Fuehrer* and Chancellor of the Reich is empowered to release anyone from the provisions of these administrative decrees.

II. The Law for the Protection of German Blood and Honor, September 15, 1935

Imbued with the knowledge that the purity of German blood is the necessary prerequisite for the existence of the German nation, and inspired by an inflexible will to maintain the existence of the German nation for all future times, the Reichstag has unanimously adopted the following law, which is now proclaimed:

ARTICLE 1. (1) Any marriages between Jews and citizens of German or kindred blood are herewith forbidden. Marriages entered into despite this law are invalid, even if they are arranged abroad as a means of circumventing this law.

(2) Annulment proceedings for marriages may be initiated only by the Public Prosecutor.

ARTICLE 2. Extramarital relations between Jews and citizens of German or kindred blood are herewith forbidden.

ARTICLE 3. Jews are forbidden to employ as servants in their households female subjects of German or kindred blood who are under the age of 45 years.

ARTICLE 4. (1) Jews are prohibited from displaying the Reich and national flag and from showing the national colors.

(2) However, they may display the Jewish colors. The exercise of this right is under State protection. . . .

ARTICLE 7. This law shall go into effect on the day following its promulgation, with the exception of Article 3, which shall go into effect on January 1, 1936.

— Reading No. 45 —

GÖRING'S BUTTER-OR GUNS SPEECH, 1936*

The nihilistic, all-or-nothing-at-all philosophy of National Socialism was expressed by Hermann Göring in this passage from a speech delivered in 1936.

Party comrades, friends . . . I have come to talk to you about Germany, about our Germany. *Germany must have a place in the sun!* But rearmament is only the first step to make the German people happy! Rearming for me is not an aim in itself. I do not want to arm for militaristic ends or to oppress other peoples, but solely for the freedom of Germany! *Meine Volksgenossen,* I am for international understanding. That is why we are rearming. Weak—we are at the mercy of the world. What is the use of being in the concert of nations if Germany is only allowed to play a comb!

I must speak clearly. Some people in international life are very hard of hearing. They can only be made to listen if they hear the guns go off. . . . We have no butter, *meine Volksgenossen,* but I ask you—would you rather have butter or guns? Shall we import lard or metal ores? Let me tell you—preparedness makes us powerful. Butter merely makes us fat!

* Quoted in Willy Frischauer, *The Rise and Fall of Hermann Goering* (Boston, 1951) p. 123.

— Reading No. 46 —

THE HOSSBACH DOCUMENT, NOVEMBER 5, 1937*

At a secret meeting held on November 5, 1937, Hitler outlined to his military leaders the practical steps in undertaking aggression against other countries. The minutes of the meeting, as recorded by Hitler's adjutant, Colonel Hossbach, reveal how Hitler planned to wage war two years before the outbreak of hostilities.

◢ ◢ ◢

The *Fuehrer* then stated: The aim of German policy is the security and the preservation of the *Volk* and its propagation. This is consequently a problem of space. . . . The question for Germany is where the greatest possible conquest can be made at lowest cost.

German politics must reckon with its two hateful enemies, England and France, to whom a strong German colossus in the center of Europe would be intolerable. Both these states would oppose a further reinforcement of Germany, both in Europe and overseas, and in this opposition they would have the support of all parties. . . .

If the *Fuehrer* is still living, then it will be his irrevocable decision to solve the German space-problem no later than 1943-45. . . . For the improvement of our military political position it must be our first aim, in every case of entanglement by war, to conquer Czechoslovakia and Austria simultaneously, in order to remove any threat from the flanks in case of a possible advance westward. . . . Once Czechoslovakia is conquered—and a

* From *Proceedings of the International Military Tribunal, Trial of the Major War Criminals* (Nuremberg, 1947-49) as quoted in G. M. Gilbert, *Psychology of Dictatorship* (New York, 1950) pp. 99-100.

mutual frontier of Germany-Hungary is obtained—then a neutral attitude by Poland in a German-French conflict could be more easily relied upon. Our agreements with Poland remain valid only as long as Germany's strength remains unshakeable. . . .

Military preparation by Russia must be countered by the speed of our operations; it is a question whether this needs to be taken into consideration at all, in view of Japan's attitude. . . .

— Reading No. 47 —

WAR SONG AGAINST ENGLAND, 1940*

This war-song, composed in 1940, was a streamlined version of the old Hasslied *of World War I.*

We challenge the lion of England,
For the last and decisive cup.
We judge and we say
An Empire breaks up.
This sure is our proudest day.
Comrade, Comrade,
The orders are here, we start right away

Go, get on, get on,
The motto is known;
Get on to the foe, get on to the foe.
BOMBS ON ENGLAND!

Listen to the engine singing—get on to the foe!
Listen, in your ears it's ringing—get on to the foe.
BOMBS, OH BOMBS, OH BOMBS ON ENGLAND!

* *Patriotic German Song, 1940, by H. Niels.*

— Reading No. 48 —

HITLER'S POLITICAL TESTAMENT, APRIL 29, 1945 *

Although before his death Hitler denounced the German people as not worthy of his leadership, he left a political testament, urging them to carry on his ideals.

✓   ✓   ✓

More than thirty years have passed since I made my modest contribution as a volunteer in the First World War, which was forced upon the Reich.

In these three decades, love and loyalty to my people alone have guided me in all my thoughts, actions, and life. They gave me power to make the most difficult decisions which have ever confronted mortal man. I have spent all my time, my powers, and my health in these three decades.

It is untrue that I or anybody else in Germany wanted war in 1939. It was wanted and provoked exclusively by those international statesmen who either were of Jewish origin or worked for Jewish interests. . . .

After six years of war, which, in spite of all setbacks, will one day go down in history as the most glorious and heroic manifestation of the struggle for existence of a nation, I cannot forsake the city that is the capital of this state. . . .

I have therefore decided to remain in Berlin and there to choose death voluntarily at that moment when I believe that the position of the *Fuehrer* and the Chancellery itself can no longer be maintained. I die with a joyful heart in my knowledge of the immeasurable deeds and achievements of our soldiers at the front, of our women at home, the achievements of our peasants and workers

* *The New York Times,* December 31, 1945.

and of a contribution unique in history, of our youth that bears my name. . . .

Before my death, I expel the former Reich Marshal Hermann Göring from the party and withdraw from him all the rights that were conferred on him by the decree of 29 June, 1941, and by my Reichstag speech of the first of September, 1939. . . .

Apart altogether from their disloyalty to me, Göring and Himmler have brought irreparable shame on the country and the whole nation by secretly negotiating with the enemy without my knowledge and against my will, and also by illegally attempting to seize control of the state.

In order to give the German people a government composed of honorable men who will fulfill the task of continuing the war with all means, as the leader of the nation I appoint the following members of the new Cabinet:

President, Doenitz; Chancellor, Dr. Goebbels; Party Minister, Bormann; Foreign Minister, Seyss-Inquart (*et al.*) . . .

— Reading No. 49 —

EXTRACTS FROM THE NUREMBERG TRIAL JUDGMENTS, OCTOBER 1, 1946*

The public trial of twenty-two Nazi leaders began at Nuremberg in November, 1948. Although special courts had been set up in the past to judge political crimes by extraordinary authority, no such court had ever obtained such universal recognition. Here was in effect the first

* Condensed from the official text in *Trial of the Major War Criminals before the International Military Tribunal* (Nuremberg, 1948) XXII, pp. 524-33, 539-41, 552-56, 556-71.

step in the creation of an international court to judge crimes against peace, against humanity, and against defenseless minorities. The legality of the proceedings troubled many jurists, who were disturbed by the ex post facto implications of the trials. But when it became clear from the carefully compiled testimony of the court how mercilessly the Nazi leaders had treated their victims, fewer and fewer voices were raised against the proceedings. The evidence showed that between five and ten million people had been starved, beaten, and tortured to death in concentration camps, a crime without parallel in history.

✦   ✦   ✦

GÖRING: From the moment he joined the party in 1922 and took command of the street fighting organization, the SA, Göring was the adviser, the active agent of Hitler and one of the prime leaders of the Nazi movement. As Hitler's political deputy he was largely instrumental in bringing the National Socialists to power in 1933, and was charged with consolidating this power and expanding the German armed might. He developed the Gestapo and created the first concentration camps, relinquishing them to Himmler in 1934; conducted the Röhm purge in that year and engineered the sordid proceedings which resulted in the removal of Von Blomberg and Von Fritsch from the army. . . .

Göring commanded the Luftwaffe in the attack on Poland and throughout the aggressive wars which followed. . . . The record is filled with Göring's admissions of his complicity in the use of slave labor. . . .

There is nothing to be said in mitigation. . . . His guilt is unique in its enormity. The record discloses no excuse for this man.

VERDICT: GUILTY on all four counts.

SENTENCE: Death by hanging.

HESS: . . . As deputy to the *Fuehrer*, Hess was the top man in the Nazi party with responsibility for handling all Party matters and authority to make decisions in Hitler's name on all questions of Party leadership. . . . Hess was an informed and willing participant in German aggression against Austria, Czechoslovakia, and Poland. . . . With him on his flight to England, Hess carried certain peace proposals which he alleged Hitler was prepared to accept. It is significant to note that this flight took place only ten days after the date on which Hitler fixed the time for attacking the Soviet Union. . . .

VERDICT: GUILTY on counts 1 and 2.

SENTENCE: Life imprisonment.

ROSENBERG: Recognized as the Party's Ideologist, he developed and spread Nazi doctrines in the newspapers *Völkischer Beobachter* and *NS Monatshefte,* which he edited, and in the numerous books he wrote. . . .

VERDICT: GUILTY on all four counts.

SENTENCE: Death by hanging.

RIBBENTROP: Ribbentrop was not present at the Hossbach Conference held on November 5, 1937, but on January 2, 1938, while Ambassador to England, he sent a memorandum to Hitler indicating his opinion that a change in the *status quo* in the East in the German sense could only be carried out by force and suggesting methods to prevent England and France from intervening in a European war fought to bring about such a change. . . .

He played an important part in Hitler's "final solution" of the Jewish question. In September, 1942, he ordered the German diplomatic representatives accredited to various satellites to hasten deportation of the Jews to the East. . . . It was because Hitler's policy and plans coincided with his own ideas that Ribbentrop served him so willingly to the end.

VERDICT: GUILTY on all four counts.

SENTENCE: Death by hanging.

— Reading No. 50 —

OCCUPATION STATUTE FOR WEST GERMANY, APRIL 8, 1949*

Following is the Occupation Statute defining the powers to be retained by the Occupation authorities in West Germany. Agreed upon in Washington by the Foreign Ministers of the Allied Powers, the statute was declared by the Allied High Commission to have entered into force as from September 21, 1949.

1. During the period in which it is necessary that the occupation continue, the Governments of France, the United States, and the United Kingdom desire and intend that the German people shall enjoy self-government to the maximum possible degree consistent with such occupation. The Federal State and the participating Laender (States) shall have, subject only to the limitations in this instrument, full legislative, executive, and judicial powers in accordance with the Basic Law and with their respective constitutions.

2. In order to ensure the accomplishment of the basic purposes of the occupation, powers in the following fields are specifically reserved, including the right to request and verify information and statistics needed by the Occupation Authorities:

   (a) Disarmament and demilitarization, including related fields of scientific research, prohibitions and restrictions on industry, and civil aviation;

* Office of the U.S. High Commissioner for Germany, *Report on Germany, September 21-December 31, 1949* (Washington, 1950) pp. 56-57.

(b) Controls in regard to the Ruhr, restitution, reparations, decartelization, deconcentration, non-discrimination in trade matters, foreign interests in Germany and claims against Germany;

(c) Foreign affairs, including international agreements made by or on behalf of Germany. . . .

3. It is the hope and expectation of the Governments of France, the United States, and the United Kingdom that the Occupation Authorities will not have occasion to take action in fields other than those specifically reserved above. The Occupation Authorities, however, reserve the right, acting under instructions of their Governments, to resume in whole or in part the exercise of full authority if they consider that to do so is essential to security or to preserve democratic government in Germany or in pursuance of the international obligations of their Governments. Before so doing they will formally advise the appropriate German authorities of their decision and the reasons therefor. . . .

8. Any action shall be deemed to be the act of the Occupation Authorities under the powers herein reserved, and effective as such under this instrument, when taken or evidenced in any matter provided by any agreement between them. The Occupation Authorities may in their discretion effectuate their decisions either directly or through instructions to the appropriate German authorities.

9. After 12 months and in any event within 18 months of the effective date of this instrument the Occupying Powers will undertake a review of its provisions in the light of experience with its operation and with a view to extending the jurisdiction of the German authorities in the legislative, executive, and judicial fields.

RECOMMENDED READING

Barraclough, G., *The Origins of Modern Germany*, 1947.

Bismarck, Otto von, *Reflections and Reminiscences*, 1899.

Brady, R. A., *The Spirit and Structure of German Fascism*, 1937.

Butler, R., *The Roots of National Socialism*, 1942.

Daniels, H. G., *The Rise of the German Republic*, 1928.

Ebenstein, W., *The Nazi State*, 1943.

Flenley, Ralph, *Modern German History*, 1953.

Goerlitz, W., *History of the German General Staff*, 1953.

Hartshorne, E. Y., *German Universities and National Socialism*, 1937.

Heiden, K., *A History of National Socialism*, 1937.

Hoover, C. B., *Germany Enters the Third Reich*, 1933.

Janowsky, O. I., and Fagen, M. M., *International Aspects of German Racial Policies*, 1937.

Kantorowicz, E., *Frederick II, 1194-1250*, 1931.

Lamprecht, K., *Deutsche Geschichte*, 16 vols., 1920-1922.

Lichtenberger, H., *The Third Reich*, 1937.

Luehr, E., *The New German Republic*, 1929.

Lutz, R. H., *The German Revolution, 1918-1919*, 1922.

Meinecke, F., *Weltbürgertum und Nationalstaat*, 7th ed., 1928.

Nowen, R., *German Theories of the Corporative State*, 1947.

Oncken, H., *Napoleon III and the Rhine*, 1928.

Pinson, Koppel S., *Modern Germany: Its History and Civilization*, 1954.

Pollock, J. K. and H. Thomas, *Germany in Power and Eclipse*, 1952.

Rauschning, H., *The Revolution of Nihilism*, 1939.

Roberts, S. H., *The House that Hitler Built*, 1937.

Rosenberg, A., *History of the German Republic*, 1936.

Schnabel, F., *Deutsche Geschichte im neunzehnten Jahrhundert*, 4 vols., 1948-1951.

Snyder, L. L., *German Nationalism: The Tragedy of a People*, 1952.

Steinberg, S. H., *A Short History of Germany*, 1945.

Sybel, H. von, *The Founding of the German Empire by William I*, 1890.

Taylor, A. J. P., *The Course of German History*, 1946.

Taylor, T., *Sword and Swastika*, 1952.

Townsend, M., *The Rise and Fall of Germany's Colonial Empire, 1884-1918*, 1930.

Treitschke, H. von, *A History of Germany in the Nineteenth Century*, 1915-1917.

Valentin, V., *The German People*, 1946.

Wallich, H. C., *Mainsprings of the German Revival*, 1955.

Wheeler-Bennett, J. W., *The Nemesis of Power*, 1953.

Ziemer, G., *Education for Death*, 1941.

INDEX

188